PSYCHOLOGY OF FINANCIAL PLANNING: PRACTITIONER'S TOOLKIT

DR. BRAD KLONTZ, CFP®
DR. CHARLES CHAFFIN
DR. TED KLONTZ

WILEY

Published by John Wiley & Sons, Inc., Hoboken, New Jersey.
Published simultaneously in Canada.

For general information on our other products and services or for technical support, please contact our Customer Care Department within the United States at (800) 762-2974, outside the United States at (317) 572-3993 or fax (317) 572-4002.

Wiley also publishes its books in a variety of electronic formats. Some content that appears in print may not be available in electronic formats. For more information about Wiley products, visit our web site at www.wiley.com.

Library of Congress Cataloging-in-Publication Data:

Names: Klontz, Brad, author. | Chaffin, Charles R., author. | Klontz, Ted, author.
Title: Psychology of financial planning : practitioner's toolkit / Dr. Brad Klontz, CFP, Dr. Charles Chaffin, Dr. Ted Klontz.
Description: Hoboken, New Jersey : John Wiley & Sons, Inc., [2023] | Includes index.
Identifiers: LCCN 2022040961 (print) | LCCN 2022040962 (ebook) | ISBN 9781394153343 (paperback) | ISBN 9781394161232 (adobe pdf) | ISBN 9781394161249 (epub)
Subjects: LCSH: Finance, Personal—Psychological aspects. | Financial security.
Classification: LCC HG179 .K5738 2023 (print) | LCC HG179 (ebook) | DDC 332.024—dc23/eng/20220923
LC record available at https://lccn.loc.gov/2022040961
LC ebook record available at https://lccn.loc.gov/2022040962

Cover Design: Wiley
Cover Image: © VectorMine/Shutterstock (modified by Wiley)

Contents

Introduction

Many of us know what we should be doing around money, but we fail to put this knowledge into action. Consider the following examples:

- Our epidemic of overspending and undersaving
- Buying when the market is high and selling when it is low, doing the exact opposite of what's in their best interest
- Trying to get rich quick
- A lack of diversification
- Saying they want one thing but failing to follow through
- Having trust issues around money
- Blowing a bonus, inheritance, lottery win, or even a big sports contract
- Failing to put a Will or Trust into place
- Getting rid of money out of feelings of guilt
- Providing financial support to adult children when the client can't afford it and/ or the children misuse the money
- Having trouble saying "no" to requests for money from family and friends, even when they know they should
- Chronic money conflicts with spouses, partners, and family members
- Lying about, or hiding, financial actions from a partner or spouse around money
- Failing to follow through on financial advice, even when they requested it
- Feeling too anxious to spend money even when they can afford to

- Sacrificing health, relationships, and emotional well-being in the pursuit of more, even when by all objective evidence they have enough

- Avoidance around money issues

- A lack of motivation, creativity, and passion in occupational pursuits

Many of these difficulties are due not to a lack of financial literacy, but to a client's psychological conditioning. As such, a basic knowledge of a client's financial psychology – their instincts, biases, beliefs, and behaviors – is essential to provide comprehensive, effective financial planning services. As technology advances and many financial services are becoming more and more commoditized, it has never been more important for financial planners to demonstrate their value in helping improve clients' financial lives. With the inclusion of the psychology of financial planning in the list of topics financial planners need to know, the field has evolved to serve clients more holistically. This evolution is less an aspirational call to action and more a recognition of the critical role financial planners have been playing in their clients' lives for decades. Including psychology in financial planning helps equip financial planners with a better understanding of their clients' values and attitudes and provides the tools they need to be better communicators and to help their clients manage money conflicts and navigate crisis events.

About This Book

This book is designed to be a companion to *Psychology of Financial Planning: The Practitioner's Guide to Money and Behavior*. Here we focus on *applying* the knowledge, tools, and techniques from the book into action. Our approach throughout both books, as well as in our education programs, is not to learn theory for the sake of defining terms (or earning continuing education credit), but rather, to help advisors learn new tools and refine old ones to help engage their clients in more meaningful ways. In each chapter we include a basic overview of the content so that you don't need to constantly flip back and forth between the two books. However, deeper explanations and contexts are provided in *Psychology of Financial Planning: The Practitioner's Guide to Money and Behavior*.

The Practitioner's Toolkit is designed with over 50 assessments and reflection exercises. You may find it more rewarding to complete many of the exercises with a colleague, sharing the results and brainstorming about ways that you can refine your work and impact your clients. If you are a student, all of the exercises and scenarios that are part of this book can help you in developing your "toolbox" of skills and techniques. We also strongly encourage you to do these exercises yourself. This will not only increase your level of confidence in using the techniques, but reflecting on your own financial psychology will have a positive impact on how you engage your clients in the future. Regardless of where you are in your professional journey, we hope that both of these books give you the knowledge and tools you need to build deeper and more effective relationships with each of the clients you serve.

To help you learn new approaches and refine old ones, we must first begin with a bit of a self-assessment. That self-assessment spans two different areas. First, it is an assessment of elements of your current practice, questioning what is working as it relates to communication, cultural competence, and getting your clients to take action. Second, and perhaps more importantly, the self-assessment helps you take an honest look at your own biases and worldview; specifically, your relationship with money and your financial beliefs and behaviors. Your financial psychology will have a profound impact on your work as a planner. Self-awareness is critical in making you an even more effective financial planner. Written as a companion to *Psychology of Financial Planning: The Practitioner's Guide to Money and Behavior,* this book focuses on the application of the tools, assessments, and reflections provided here that will help you with everything from deepening your sense of cultural humility to helping you get your clients to take action.

We are all planners. So as you work through this toolkit, we invite you to document what you learn about yourself as an individual and as a planner; opportunities for your firm to improve; and where you would like to see your practice in the near and distant future. The results of these discoveries can create a living document for you and your firm and, hopefully, a toolbox of knowledge, reflection, and techniques that can only improve your impact and, most importantly, the lives of your clients.

As the field continues to evolve, so does our understanding of the psychology of financial planning. For the latest developments make sure to visit us at www .psychologyoffinancialplanning.com.

How to Use This Book

This book is designed to help you (or your firm or, if you are a student, your class) better understand yourself – specifically, your biases, experiences, and background and how all of those impact the lens that you bring to your current or future practice. There are a series of assessments and reflection exercises that require you to seriously consider the worldview that you bring to your clients. We have included exercises that can be used with clients, and we encourage you to complete them first on your own. Readers may also find it helpful to share some of their experiences and self-discoveries with a colleague, classmate, or loved one.

Although we provide short overviews of main topics that impact the exercises, we recommend that you consult *Psychology of Financial Planning: The Practitioner's Guide to Money and Behavior* for additional tools, full definitions, and a broader context around the topics.

Chapter 1

Client Values and Goals

In this chapter, we provide tools that you can use with clients to help them gain clarity around their values and goals. But before we do that, let's focus on what drives you in your professional and/or educational pursuits.

Exercise 1: What Drives You?

Spend some time thinking about what motivates you in your practice. Consider your mindset when you start work each day. What drives you to work a little harder than you otherwise would? Maybe it is related to providing for your family or maybe it is a desire to profoundly impact the lives of your clients. Perhaps you are a student and you are excited about the prospect of helping others through financial planning. Take a few minutes and outline what drives you in your career.

_____

_____

_____

_____

_____

_____

_____

_____

_____

Look back on what you wrote. Were your motivations more extrinsic (focused on rewards and money) or intrinsic (internal rewards for the sake of doing them)? For many of us it is a combination of both. Have your motivations evolved over time?

Most human behavior can be explained by a basic set of needs. Our needs affect our behaviors. We have fundamental physiological needs, such as food, water, and rest, and they can take priority if they are not being met. Think about when you are hungry. The thought of food can dominate your work and interaction with others. As financial planners, understanding what motivates human behavior and its relationship to our goals enables us to help clients develop and achieve their own goals.

Exercise 2: Tape Measure Exercise

The tape measure exercise is designed to assess one's values and goals and can be used as a motivational tool. It can be a very powerful emotional experience. Following the intervention, clients may feel a sense of excitement, hope, sadness, or remorse. Regardless, the intervention can be used to help clients take an honest and realistic look at their financial status, affirm their successes, grieve their losses, gain clarity on what matters most to them, and take action on meeting their financial goals.

Materials Needed

(1) A soft tailor/seamstress tape measure (e.g., 120 inches) and (2) a pair of scissors

Instructions

For this exercise, complete the following seven steps:

Step 1. How old are you?

From the bottom of the tape measure, find your age (e.g., 45). Cut this from the bottom of the tape measure (e.g., the first 45 inches). This is the past. It is done. Hold this piece of tape in your hands. What thoughts or feelings arise about these years? Throw this piece of tape away. Notice any thoughts or feelings that emerge.

Step 2. What is your life expectancy?

Historically, how old do people in your family live (e.g., 95)? Adjust up or down depending on your health status compared to others in your family, taking modern medicine into account. Cut this from the top of the tape measure (e.g., at 95 inches). Throw this piece of tape away. What thoughts or feelings arise about these years?

Step 3. What remains in your hands is the life you have left, assuming everything goes well.

What thoughts or feelings arise as you hold this tape in your hands? What do you want to do with these years? What matters most to you?

Step 4. What age do you want to "retire"?

In other words, at what age do you want to have financial freedom? That is, where you don't need to rely on work to produce income to live at your financial comfort level of choice; where you can do what you want to do, whenever you want to do it. This could be retirement or just continuing to work without a need for income. Cut this from the top of the tape measure (e.g., at 65 inches).

Step 5. Now look at the years you have between now and retirement.

Compare this piece of tape to the tape representing the number of years you will be retired. What thoughts or feelings arise from these two pieces of tape? What do you need to do between now and retirement to make sure you can fund your retirement years?

Step 6. Identify three positive takeaways from this exercise. What are you most pleased with? What are you most proud of?

1. _____

2. _____

3. _____

Step 7. Identify three action steps that emerge from this exercise. What is missing in your life? What do you need to change? What steps do you need to take? What are you committed to doing?

1. _____

2. _____

3. _____

Exercise 3: Incomplete Sentences Intervention

This exercise is designed for self-discovery. Since it is estimated that at least 90% of all decisions are made subconsciously, methods such as these can be more efficient at discovering a client's authentic values. Simply asking a client what they value primarily engages the prefrontal cortex, which is relatively inefficient in terms of eliciting data that will create motivation for change. Often what truly motivates and inspires us most lies below our conscious awareness.

Instructions

Imagine that you were able to receive a letter from a descendant of yours. They have asked you to share with them your answers to the questions below. Answer each one with a sentence or two.

1. How did you feel about your life?

   _____

   _____

   _____

   _____

   _____

   _____

_____

_____

_____

_____

2. What were the most important lessons you learned?

_____

_____

_____

_____

_____

_____

_____

_____

_____

3. What did you wish you had done that you didn't do?

_____

_____

_____

_____

_____

_____

_____

Client Values and Goals

_____

_____

_____

_____

4. What are you really glad you experienced/accomplished?

_____

_____

_____

_____

_____

_____

_____

_____

_____

_____

5. What kinds of things touched your heart?

_____

_____

_____

_____

_____

_____

_____

_____

_____

_____

6. What kinds of things moved you to tears?

_____

_____

_____

_____

_____

_____

_____

_____

7. What kinds of things outraged you?

_____

_____

_____

_____

_____

_____

_____

8. What frightened you?

_____

_____

_____

_____

_____

_____

_____

_____

_____

_____

9. What excited you?

_____

_____

_____

_____

_____

_____

_____

_____

Psychology of Financial Planning: Practitioner's Toolkit

10. What made you smile?

11. What was special about those you loved?

Client Values and Goals

12. What advice would you give a young person like me?

13. What did you learn about human nature?

_____

_____

_____

14. What did you learn about the meaning of life?

_____

_____

_____

_____

_____

_____

_____

_____

_____

15. What were your money beliefs?

_____

_____

_____

_____

_____

_____

_____

_____

_____

_____

Using these answers, draft a three- to four-sentence paragraph that represents your legacy statement. Consider sharing your legacy statement with someone close to you, whether a partner or colleague.

_____

_____

_____

_____

_____

_____

_____

_____

_____

_____

Exercise 4: Self-Efficacy Reflection

Self-efficacy is the core belief in our ability to succeed in a given situation or context and has a great impact on how we think, behave, and feel.[1] A sense of confidence in one's ability to successfully tackle a challenge is an important precondition for making changes.

Think back to when you faced a significant challenge. Did you find the resolve to meet that challenge or were you more prone to give up and walk away?

In that situation, what was the biggest determinant of whether you "went for it" or surrendered?

The financial planner can also take large goals and break them into smaller, more manageable steps. Throughout that process, the planner can check in with the client and celebrate the small successes to remind the client that they are making progress and are on track to meet their larger goal. The planner could also take time to address any potential barriers to achieving client goals and discuss them. As always, avoiding jargon and being very specific regarding next steps is critical, as the planner wants to do everything in their power to make clients' financial self-efficacy as simple and straightforward as possible.

Note

1. Bandura, A. (Ed.). (1995). *Self-Efficacy in Changing Societies.* [online] Cambridge, UK: Cambridge University Press. doi:10.1017/cbo9780511527692.

Chapter 2

Multicultural Competence in Financial Planning

Our clients have diverse backgrounds, worldviews, and experiences that impact the financial planning process and the client–planner relationship. We should consider examining the ways clients are influenced by their own cultural identity and their minority and majority status across some important categories within their culture. The better a financial planner understands their own cultural identity, the more they will become aware of the biases and assumptions that can impact their work with clients. Becoming aware of how our own lived experiences differ from those of others will help increase our empathy and effectiveness.

Exercise 5: Your Multicultural Experience

In the space below, identify your own exposure to individuals of different cultural backgrounds. This could have been through travel, education, or another personal experience. How have those experiences impacted you?

_____

_____

_____

_____

_____

_____

_____

_____

_____

_____

Exercise 6: Your Current (or Future) Clientele

How diverse are your current clients? Have you had success in engaging clients with diverse backgrounds or have you struggled to retain clients who are different from you and other members of your firm? If you are a student, do you feel adequately prepared to engage individuals with different backgrounds than you?

_____

_____

_____

_____

_____

_____

_____

_____

_____

Majority and Minority Status That Impact Financial Planning

We are all vulnerable to biases that grow out of our own backgrounds. We also tend to categorize and generalize, which can contribute to inaccurate assumptions about others. Majority group members – as defined by historical power and influence within a culture – may have difficulty noticing their own biases because their worldview may be widely held within the culture. This is often referred to as "majority group privilege." Meanwhile, a member of a minority group may be more sensitive to how their worldview and experiences are different from the dominant culture. As financial planners, a recognition of our own cultural identity and any biases that come from it can make us more sensitive to those who are different from us. This can make us more effective in understanding our clients' experiences, needs, and goals.

Exercise 7: ADDRESSING Exercise

The ADDRESSING exercise is a great way for planners to better understand their own worldview and biases as well as understand those who are different from them in some way.[1] Depending on the country in which you reside, your cultural identity will fall into either the majority status or minority status in several areas. The following chart is adapted from the work of Dr. Pamela Hays,[2,3] and is a useful tool for exploring one's majority and minority status. Within each category, someone in the majority status may have access to different experiences and/or special advantages, while someone with minority status may have less power within the culture and therefore experience additional obstacles and challenges.

The ADDRESSING acronym stands for:

Cultural Identity	Majority Status (in the United States)	Minority Status (in the United States)
Age and generational influences	Adults	Children, adolescents, elders
Developmental disability	Able-bodied/mentally healthy	Individuals born with disabilities
Disability (acquired later in life)	Able-bodied/mentally healthy	Individuals with physical and/or mental disabilities
Religion and spiritual orientation	Christian	Non-Christian

(continued)

Multicultural Competence in Financial Planning

Cultural Identity	Majority Status (in the United States)	Minority Status (in the United States)
Ethnicity/race identity	White or Caucasian	Persons of color
Socioeconomic status	Middle class or higher	Lower income
Sexual orientation	Heterosexual	Gay, lesbian, bisexual
Indigenous heritage	Non-native	Native
National origin	U.S.-born	Immigrants, refugees, international students
Gender	Male	Women, transgender, nonbinary, intersex

A useful exercise in understanding your own cultural identity is to go through each of these categories and self-identify. Put a check in the appropriate box that identifies you as a member of the majority or minority culture in the ADDRESSING categories.

Cultural Identity	Majority Status (in the United States)	Minority Status (in the United States)
Age and generational influences		
Developmental disability		
Disability (acquired later in life)		
Religion and spiritual orientation		
Ethnicity/race identity		
Socioeconomic status		
Sexual orientation		
Indigenous heritage		

Cultural Identity	Majority Status (in the United States)	Minority Status (in the United States)
National origin		
Gender		

In completing the ADDRESSING exercise, consider the following questions:

How was this experience for you?

_____

_____

_____

_____

_____

_____

_____

_____

_____

Did anything surprise you?

_____

_____

_____

_____

_____

_____

_____

_____

_____

How has your minority/majority status in these areas impacted your life experiences, financial or otherwise?

_____

_____

_____

_____

_____

_____

_____

_____

_____

How might a client's minority/majority status in these areas impact their life experiences, financial or otherwise?

_____

_____

_____

_____

_____

_____

_____

_____

_____

_____

How have one or more aspects of your cultural identity impacted your relationship with money?

_____

_____

_____

_____

_____

_____

_____

_____

_____

Does this experience impact the short- or long-term planning of your firm? If so, how and who needs to be involved?

_____

_____

_____

_____

_____

_____

_____

_____

_____

_____

Notes

1. Hays, P., Klontz, B. T., and Kemnitz, R. (2015). Seven steps to culturally responsive financial therapy. In B. T. Klontz, S. L. Britt, and K. L. Archuleta (Eds.), *Financial Therapy: Theory, Research and Practice* (pp. 151–172). New York, NY: Springer.
2. Ibid.
3. Hays, P. A. (2001). *Addressing Cultural Complexities in Practice: A Framework for Clinicians and Counselors*. Washington, DC: American Psychological Association.

Chapter 3

Financial Flashpoints: Exploring a Client's Financial Background

Financial flashpoints are life events "associated with money that are so emotionally powerful, they leave an imprint that lasts into adulthood."[1] Financial flashpoints can range from the mundane to the traumatic and are a key element in the development of our financial psychology (as illustrated in Figure 3.1).[2] In our attempt to make sense of our experiences, we develop money scripts®, which drive our financial behaviors. Our financial behaviors and outcomes, in turn, give rise to new financial flashpoint experiences, which either further ingrain our money scripts or inspire us to adapt and change them. An exploration of an individual's financial flashpoints can provide important clues around how they have shaped their relationship with money. In fact, even some of the most befuddling

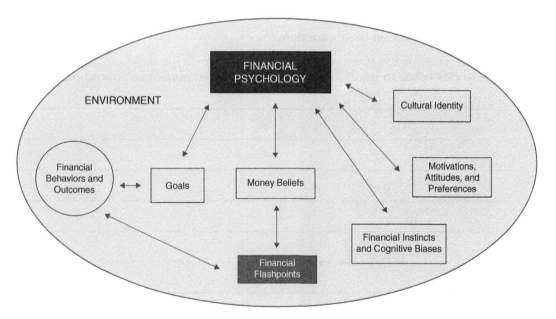

Figure 3.1   Klontz-Chaffin Model of Financial Psychology

financial behaviors can make perfect sense when a financial planner understands the circumstances that shaped the client's mindset around money. Connecting the dots between a client's financial past and their present can help them more consciously create the financial future they want and anticipate potential psychological roadblocks along the way. Financial flashpoints can have intense emotions around them, and in some cases, lasting change might require a referral to a therapist with experience in working with trauma.

The following exercises are designed to help individuals identify their financial flashpoints and explore their impact on the development of their unique financial psychology. Some of these questions can be seamlessly woven into conversations with clients, while others offer deeper dives that might be more typically administered in a financial coaching engagement. Regardless, all financial professionals could benefit from completing the following exercise to increase their awareness of their own financial psychology.

Exercise 8: Your Ancestral Flashpoints

Reflect on the following questions related to the experiences of your parents, grandparents, and great-grandparents around money and how it impacts their financial psychology. It can be helpful to interview, if possible, your parents, grandparents, and/or other family members to help you have a deeper understanding of the financial beliefs you have inherited based on their experiences.

- What stories come to mind about your ancestors' experiences around money?

_____

_____

_____

_____

_____

_____

_____

_____

_____

_____

- Were your ancestors immigrants? If so, did their immigrant status somehow impact their relationship with money?

_____

_____

_____

_____

_____

_____

_____

_____

- How did their culture of origin shape their financial experiences?

_____

_____

_____

_____

_____

_____

_____

_____

_____

- What beliefs around money did they adopt to make sense of these experiences?

_____

_____

_____

_____

_____

_____

_____

_____

_____

_____

Exercise 9: Your Financial Flashpoints

The experiences of those who came before us shape our relationship with money. Our individual experiences do the same. Spend some time reflecting on the following questions.

Your Childhood Experiences

- What is your earliest memory around money?

_____

_____

_____

_____

_____

_____

_____

_____

_____

_____

- What is your most joyful money memory?

_____

_____

_____

_____

_____

_____

_____

_____

_____

- What is your most painful memory around money?

_____

_____

_____

_____

_____

Financial Flashpoints: Exploring a Client's Financial Background

_____

_____

_____

_____

_____

- What beliefs around money did you adopt to make sense of these experiences?

_____

_____

_____

_____

_____

_____

_____

_____

_____

_____

Socioeconomic Status

- What was your socioeconomic status growing up?

_____

_____

_____

_____

_____

_____

_____

_____

_____

_____

- How did you feel about it? Were you proud, ashamed, or somewhere in between?

_____

_____

_____

_____

_____

_____

_____

_____

_____

_____

- How did it impact your day-to-day experiences for better or worse?

_____

_____

_____

_____

_____

_____

_____

_____

_____

_____

- How did you see yourself as compared to others?

_____

_____

_____

_____

_____

_____

_____

_____

_____

_____

_____

- What beliefs around money did you adopt to make sense of these experiences?

_____

_____

_____

_____

_____

_____

_____

_____

_____

_____

- How did it impact your financial behaviors?

_____

_____

_____

_____

_____

_____

_____

_____

_____

_____

_____

Financial Support

- In times of financial need, did you have friends or family members you could engage for support?

_____

_____

_____

_____

_____

_____

_____

_____

_____

_____

- How did this support, or lack thereof, impact your beliefs about money?

_____

_____

_____

_____

_____

_____

_____

_____

_____

- How did it impact your financial behaviors?

_____

_____

_____

_____

_____

_____

_____

_____

_____

- What beliefs around money did you adopt to make sense of these experiences?

_____

_____

_____

_____

_____

_____

_____

_____

_____

_____

Gender

- What messages did you receive from your parents around gender and money?

  _____

  _____

  _____

  _____

  _____

  _____

  _____

  _____

  _____

  _____

- How did your gender impact your upbringing around money?

  _____

  _____

  _____

  _____

  _____

  _____

  _____

  _____

  _____

  _____

- How did your childhood experiences around money differ from those of your differently gendered siblings/cousins/friends?

_____

_____

_____

_____

_____

_____

_____

- What expectations around money, work, or family finances were put on you based on your gender?

_____

_____

_____

_____

_____

_____

_____

_____

- What beliefs around money did you adopt to make sense of these experiences?

_____

_____

_____

_____

_____

_____

_____

_____

_____

_____

Stress and Trauma

- How much stress did your family experience around money in your early years?

_____

_____

_____

_____

_____

_____

_____

_____

_____

_____

- Did your family's financial situation change dramatically at some point in your life? If so, how did that impact you?

_____

_____

_____

_____

_____

_____

_____

_____

_____

- Were you ever exposed to violence or discrimination, or have you felt judged or excluded based on your socioeconomic status?

_____

_____

_____

_____

_____

_____

_____

_____

_____

- What beliefs around money did you adopt to make sense of these experiences?

_____

_____

_____

_____

_____

_____

_____

_____

_____

_____

Cultural Events

- What experiences have you had around money that were specific to your culture, race, and/or ethnicity?

_____

_____

_____

_____

_____

_____

_____

_____

_____

_____

- What beliefs around money did you adopt to make sense of these experiences?

_____

_____

_____

_____

_____

_____

_____

_____

- How did broader economic events during your lifetime impact you (e.g., recession, inflation, war, etc.)?

_____

_____

_____

_____

_____

_____

_____

_____

_____

Exercise 10: The Money Egg

The money egg is designed to help identify our financial flashpoints.[3] It provides an opportunity to link our experiences around money to our beliefs and emotions. It can be used in individual and group settings. It is helpful to complete this exercise rather quickly in an attempt to avoid overthinking or second-guessing your impulses. Try to spend no more than 10 minutes on the first two steps:

1. On a sheet of paper, draw an egg-shaped circle (or use the one in Figure 3.2).

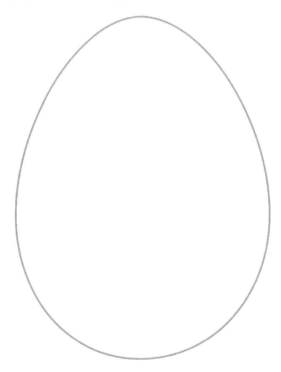

Figure 3.2   Money Egg Example: Step 1

2. Reflect on your early life. Starting at the bottom of the egg, with your nondominant hand, draw a symbol that represents the first painful and/or pleasurable experience that you had with money (see the example shown in Figure 3.3).

Psychology of Financial Planning: Practitioner's Toolkit

Figure 3.3   Money Egg Example: Step 2

3. Section this off (as illustrated in Figure 3.4) and continue up the egg with the next experience. Keep going until you reach your most recent impactful money memory.

Figure 3.4   Money Egg Example: Step 3

Financial Flashpoints: Exploring a Client's Financial Background

4. Go back and look at each symbol. Imagine each of these situations and write down a few words that describe the emotions that you felt then or feel now in relation to the experience (as illustrated in Figure 3.5). If you are not aware of having feelings (then or now), imagine you are witnessing this happening to your child or loved one. Write down your feelings as you are imagining this happening to him or her.

_____

_____

_____

_____

_____

_____

_____

_____

_____

_____

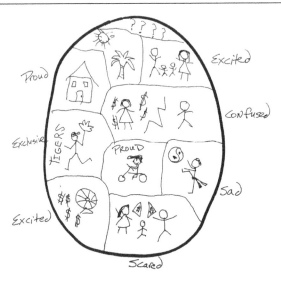

Figure 3.5   Money Egg Example: Step 4

Psychology of Financial Planning: Practitioner's Toolkit

5. Create a list of lessons that you learned about money based upon these experiences in the space below (as illustrated in Figure 3.6).

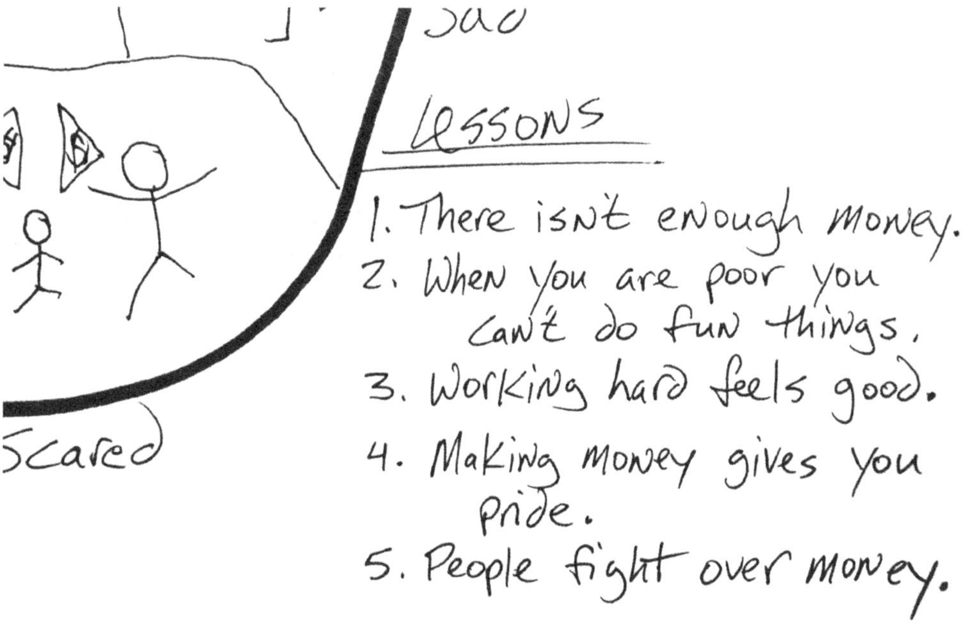

_____

_____

_____

_____

_____

_____

_____

_____

_____

_____

Figure 3.6   Money Egg Example: Step 5

6. Complete this sentence: "The moral of the story about money is . . ."

_____

_____

_____

_____

_____

_____

_____

_____

_____

_____

_____

Notes

1. Klontz, B., and Klontz T. (2009). *Mind Over Money: Overcoming the Money Disorders That Threaten Our Financial Health* (p. 8). Broadway Books.
2. Klontz, B. T., Chaffin, C. R., and Klontz, P. T. (2023). *Psychology of Financial Planning: The Practitioner's Guide to Money and Behavior*. Hoboken, NJ: Wiley.
3. Klontz, B. T., Kahler, R., and Klontz, P. T. (2016). *Facilitating Financial Health: Tools for Financial Planners, Coaches, and Therapists*. Cincinnati, OH: National Underwriters Company.

Chapter 4

Money Scripts: Exploring a Client's Beliefs About Money

In our attempts to make sense of our financial flashpoints, we develop beliefs about money called *money scripts*. Often these beliefs about money are partially true, incomplete, and conflicting, but subconsciously followed in adulthood.[1] Identifying one's money scripts can be an important part of understanding an individual's financial psychology.

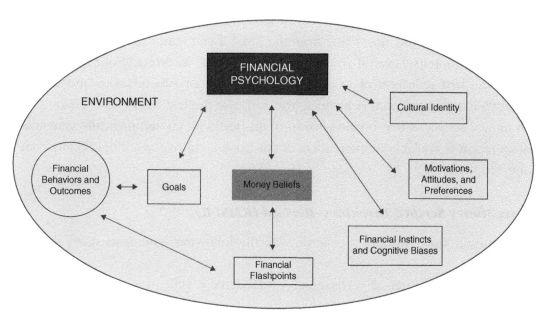

Figure 4.1   Klontz-Chaffin Model of Financial Psychology

Exercise 11: The Klontz Money Script Inventory–Revised (KMSI-R)

There is a strong link between money scripts and financial outcomes. The Klontz Money Script Inventory was developed to help people discover their money scripts. It has been researched extensively and scores on the KMSI have been found to be associated with income, net worth, credit card debt, socioeconomic status in childhood, financial behaviors, and other aspects of financial health.[2,3]

For many people, discovering and exploring their money scripts are important steps in increasing their income, net worth, and financial health. The KMSI offers a valid, efficient, and reliable tool to help measure money beliefs and attitudes.[4] In the revised version of the test, there are 32 money statements that fall into four categories: (1) money avoidance; (2) money worship (often referred to as money focus when used in a financial planning context); (3) money status; and (4) money vigilance.

To get the most value from this test, try to avoid falling prey to "social desirability," which is the psychological impulse that tells us that we must show our best selves. No one else needs to see your scores, so you have no reason to try to appear smart or perfect. You will get the most value from the KMSI if you read each statement and go with your first impulse, even if you know that it may be "incorrect." Your first impulse is likely the best reflection of what is happening in your subconscious and what is driving your actual financial behaviors. You can take the test below to examine your own money scripts. A free online version of this test with an automatically generated custom report is available to the readers of this book at: https://www.bradklontz.com/moneyscriptstest.

Klontz Money Script® Inventory–Revised (KMSI-R)

Please indicate how strongly you agree with the following statements using the following scale:

1 = Strongly Disagree, 2 = Disagree, 3 = Disagree a Little, 4 = Agree a Little, 5 = Agree, 6 = Strongly Agree

	1 Strongly Disagree	2 Disagree	3 Disagree a Little	4 Agree a Little	5 Agree	6 Strongly Agree
1. I do not deserve a lot of money when others have less than me.						
2. Rich people are greedy.						
3. I do not deserve money.						
4. Good people should not care about money.						
5. It is hard to be rich and be a good person.						
6. The less money you have, the better life is.						
7. Money corrupts people.						
8. Being rich means you no longer fit in with old friends and family.						
9. People get rich by taking advantage of others.						

(continued)

Money Scripts: Exploring a Client's Beliefs About Money

	1 Strongly Disagree	2 Disagree	3 Disagree a Little	4 Agree a Little	5 Agree	6 Strongly Agree
10. Things would get better if I had more money.						
11. More money will make you happier.						
12. It is hard to be poor and happy.						
13. You can never have enough money.						
14. Money is power.						
15. Money would solve all my problems.						
16. Money buys freedom.						
17. Most poor people do not deserve to have money.						
18. You can have love or money, but not both.						
19. I will not buy something unless it is new (e.g., car, house).						
20. Poor people are lazy.						
21. Money is what gives life meaning.						

Psychology of Financial Planning: Practitioner's Toolkit

	1 Strongly Disagree	2 Disagree	3 Disagree a Little	4 Agree a Little	5 Agree	6 Strongly Agree
22. Your self-worth equals your net worth.						
23. If something is not considered the "best," it is not worth buying.						
24. People are only as successful as the amount of money they earn.						
25. You should not tell others how much money you have or make.						
26. It is wrong to ask others how much money they have or make.						
27. Money should be saved, not spent.						
28. It is important to save for a rainy day.						
29. People should work for their money and not be given financial handouts.						

(continued)

Money Scripts: Exploring a Client's Beliefs About Money

	1 Strongly Disagree	2 Disagree	3 Disagree a Little	4 Agree a Little	5 Agree	6 Strongly Agree
30. I would be a nervous wreck if I did not have money saved for an emergency.						
31. You should always look for the best deal before buying something.						
32. It is extravagant to spend money on oneself.						

Scoring Procedures

In the following, place the point value on the line corresponding to the item. Add the points in each column and divide them by the number of items to determine the average score.

Money Avoidance	Money Worship	Money Status	Money Vigilance
1	10	17	25
2	11	18	26
3	12	19	27
4	13	20	28
5	14	21	29
6	15	22	30
7	16	23	31

Money Avoidance	Money Worship	Money Status	Money Vigilance
8		24	32
9			
Total ____ / 9 = ____	Total ____ / 7 = ____	Total ____ / 8 = ____	Total ____ / 8 = ____

Your Results

Scores on the money script scales range from 1 to 6. Higher scores indicate stronger levels of conviction in the particular category of money beliefs. It is not uncommon to have money scripts that seem at first glance to contradict each other, such as endorsing the belief that "money corrupts people" while also believing that "things would get better if I had more money."

Scoring Key:

- Scores lower than or equal to 3: Suggest you do not exhibit the money script.
- Scores between 3 and 4: Suggest you exhibit some characteristics of the money script.
- Scores higher than 4: Suggest you exhibit many of the characteristics of the money script.

Money Avoidance

Higher scores on money avoidance suggest a belief that money is bad. Money avoiders may also believe that they do not deserve money. They believe that wealthy people are greedy or corrupt, and that there is virtue in living with less money. Because of their negative associations with money and the wealthy, money avoiders may sabotage their financial success and/or give money away in an unconscious effort to stay at a comfortable socioeconomic level.

Research has found that money-avoidant beliefs are associated with lower levels of education, lower income, and lower net worth. Money avoidance is also

Money Scripts: Exploring a Client's Beliefs About Money

associated with problematic financial behaviors such as hoarding disorder, financial enabling, compulsive buying disorder, workaholism, and financial denial.[5] Young, single adults are most likely to be money-avoidant. Certain occupations, such as mental health professionals, have also been found to have higher levels of money avoidance.[6]

Money Focus

The money-focused believe that the key to happiness and the solution to their problems is to have more money. At the same time, they believe that one can never have enough money, and find that the pursuit of money never quite satisfies them. Research suggests that single, younger clients with lower levels of education and income are most vulnerable to these beliefs, while also carrying higher levels of revolving credit debt. In addition, those with money worship beliefs are more susceptible to compulsive buying disorder, hoarding disorder, workaholism, financial dependence, financial enabling, and financial denial.[7]

Money Status

Money status seekers tend to link their self-worth with their net worth. They may prioritize outward displays of wealth, and as a result can be at risk of overspending. They may believe that if they live a virtuous life, the universe will take care of their financial needs. Many have grown up in lower socioeconomic environments and/or a household that prioritized the financial aspects of social standing. Those who score higher in the area of money status are more likely to overspend, gamble excessively, be financially dependent on others, and hide expenditures from their spouses. Like the two previous categories, money status beliefs are also associated with younger, single people with lower education, income, and net worth. Those who grow up in a lower socioeconomic class have a higher likelihood of having a money status mindset, which is a predictor of compulsive buying disorder, gambling disorder, financial dependence, and financial infidelity.[8] However, wealthier individuals are also impacted by these beliefs, suggesting that the money status mindset can be a motivator to reach wealth, since self-worth is equated with net worth.[9]

Money Vigilance

The money-vigilant are alert, watchful, and concerned about their financial health. They believe it is important to save and for people to work for their money and not be given financial handouts. Those with higher money vigilance scores are positively associated with higher levels of financial health. The money-vigilant are less likely to buy on credit. They also tend to be somewhat anxious about their financial futures, inspiring them to save.

While they tend to be discreet about their financial status with others, they are less likely to keep financial secrets from their partners. While money vigilance encourages saving and frugality, it can also lead to excessive wariness or anxiety that can prevent one from enjoying the benefits and sense of security that money can provide.

Exercise 12: Money Script Log

Money scripts are those typically subconscious beliefs we have about money that drive our financial behavior.[10,11] Often they are passed down to us from our parents, grandparents, and culture. Money scripts are associated with a variety of financial outcomes, including education, income, net worth, and credit card debt[12] and drive our financial behaviors.[13]

Since our money scripts often lie outside our conscious awareness, it can help to track one's thinking outside of the office. Many of us are not aware of what happens before we engage in financial behavior. It can take some guided discovery and practice to increase our awareness of our automatic thoughts. To re-create the sequence of events, it helps to examine what happened in the moments before the behavior. To assist in this process, clients can be given a Money Script Log to complete at home.

The Money Scripts Log asks four questions:

1. *What happened (trigger)?* It is important to identify the situation, event, or emotion that prompted the behavior. Triggering events can include feelings of sadness or loneliness, a conversation with our spouse about money, opening up a

Money Scripts: Exploring a Client's Beliefs About Money

credit card statement, or watching the financial news. Cultivating an awareness of our triggers is important so we can learn to avoid them and/or prepare to counteract our automatic responses.

2. *What went through your mind (money script)?* This question forces us to essentially think about our thinking. With some practice, we can learn to observe our thinking in the moment. With some insight regarding our histories, we can learn to distinguish between helpful thoughts in the here-and-now and old money scripts that are no longer useful.

3. *What was your impulse?* This asks a client to identify what the belief compelled them to do – what action or inaction followed the money scripts?

4. *What did you do?* This tracks the actual behavior that resulted from the trigger, money script, and impulse.

The client can bring the Money Scripts Log back to the advisor's office for discussion. The Money Scripts Log can increase awareness of money scripts and help the advisor and client identify patterns.

A key objective of the Money Scripts Log is to slow down the process so that the client can gain insight into and increase control of their behavior. Typically, we move from trigger to action automatically, unconsciously, and rapidly. When we can perform a psychological autopsy on our money scripts after a financial behavior, we can identify patterns. We can learn what triggers us, patterns of thought that result, and how this leads to behaviors. We can help clients put time and space between triggers, thoughts, and actions, helping them make more conscious decisions. When these patterns become conscious, clients can insert helpful questions such as: "Is it really worth it?" "Is there something else I can do to make me feel better?" "Does this decision fit with my goals?"

Instructions

When you notice a money-related feeling or impulse, ask yourself, "What is going through my mind right now?" Then, as soon as possible, write down the situation and identify the thought or mental image in the money script column. Rate the intensity of the feeling associated with the money script on a scale of 1 to 10. In the last column, rate the feeling and its intensity after your adaptive response.

Use these questions to help you develop an adaptive response:

1. What is the evidence that the money script is true? What is the evidence that it is not true?

_____

_____

_____

_____

_____

_____

_____

_____

_____

2. Is there an alternative explanation?

_____

_____

_____

_____

_____

_____

_____

_____

_____

_____

3. What's the worst that could happen? Could I live through it? What is the best that could happen? What is the most realistic/likely outcome?

_____

_____

_____

_____

_____

_____

_____

_____

4. What's the effect of my believing this money script? What could be the effect of changing my thinking?

_____

_____

_____

_____

_____

_____

_____

_____

_____

5. What could I do about it?

_____

_____

_____

_____

_____

_____

_____

_____

_____

6. If _____ (a friend) was in the situation and had this thought, what would I tell him/her?

_____

_____

_____

_____

_____

_____

Money Scripts: Exploring a Client's Beliefs About Money

_____

_____

_____

_____

7. What is the most helpful way to think about this?

_____

_____

_____

_____

_____

_____

_____

_____

_____

_____

8. What helpful actions can I take?

_____

_____

_____

_____

_____

_____

_____

_____

_____

_____

_____

Situation	Money Script	Feeling (1–10)	Adaptive Response(s)	Feeling (1–10)
Noticed the DJIA lost 400 points today.	"I am going to lose all of my money."	Scared (8)	I am diversified so I am not going to lose all my money. I consulted with my financial planner.	Scared (4)

Exercise 13: New Money Mantra

A mantra is a word or phrase that is typically repeated over and over again. Klontz and Klontz described a money mantra methodology for overcoming self-defeating money scripts or cognitive biases.[14] The purpose is to create a financial statement that can be used to counteract and replace a money belief that is unhelpful, limiting, or self-destructive. An unhelpful money script is identified and replaced by a new, healthier, and more helpful way to think about money that is in line with an individual's values and goals. When the unhelpful money scripts arise, the new money mantra can be used to override these automatic thoughts. Over time, the unwanted money scripts begin to subside and the new, healthy thoughts emerge and strengthen.

Klontz and Klontz recommended that people write down their new money mantra and carry it with them throughout the day as a powerful tool that can help remind

Money Scripts: Exploring a Client's Beliefs About Money

them to make healthier financial choices.[15] The new money mantra can also be memorized, revisited daily in the morning and/or just before bed, or even recorded on an audio file on one's smartphone to be listened to several times a day.

Instructions

1. Identify a situation that is causing problems for you. Articulate the thoughts that come to mind in the situation and the resulting emotions.

    Example: An individual struggles with workaholism, which has been having a negative impact on his relationships and health.

    - *Situation: When I get ready to leave work.*
    - *Money scripts: "I need to work harder." "I don't have enough money." "I don't want to be seen as lazy." "I don't want to be poor."*
    - *Feelings: Anxiety, fear, guilt, shame*
    - *Situation:*

    _____

    _____

    _____

    _____

    _____

    _____

    _____

    _____

    _____

    _____

- *Money scripts:*

_____

_____

_____

_____

_____

_____

_____

_____

_____

- *Feelings:*

_____

_____

_____

_____

_____

_____

_____

_____

_____

Money Scripts: Exploring a Client's Beliefs About Money

2. Go back to the money script that underlies the feeling and rewrite several healthier more helpful self-statements.

   Example:

   - *Money scripts: "I work hard enough." "Money isn't everything; besides, I am making good money and I am on track for meeting my financial goals."*

   - *Money scripts:*

   _____

   _____

   _____

   _____

   _____

   _____

   _____

   _____

   _____

   _____

3. Identify the values that underlie these revised money scripts.

   Example:

   - *Values: Time with family, health, and a balanced life.*

   - *Values:*

   _____

   _____

   _____

_____

_____

_____

_____

_____

_____

_____

4. Create a new money mantra that reflects your revised money scripts and values.

    Example:

- *"I work hard and make good money; money isn't everything, and I am on track for meeting my financial goals. Time with family, health, and a balanced life are more important to me than accumulating money and possessions."*

- *New money mantra:*

_____

_____

_____

_____

_____

_____

_____

_____

_____

5. Keep your new money mantra close at hand. Repeat it several times each day. When you are being triggered by old money scripts that are causing you distress and keeping you from what matters most, repeat your new money mantra several times. Then check in and see how your feelings have changed and choose a behavior that is in line with your new money mantra, your values, and your goals.

_____

_____

_____

_____

_____

_____

_____

_____

_____

_____

Notes

1. Klontz, B., Britt, S. L., and Archuleta, K. L. (2015). *Financial Therapy: Theory, Research, and Practice*. Cham: Springer.
2. Klontz, B. T., and Britt, S. L. (2012). How clients' money scripts predict their financial behaviors. *Journal of Financial Planning, 25*(11), 33–43.
3. Klontz, B. T., Britt, S. L., Mentzer, J., and Klontz, T. (2011). Money beliefs and financial behaviors: Development of the Klontz Money Script Inventory. *Journal of Financial Therapy, 2*(1), 1–22.

4. Klontz, B. T., Chaffin, C. R., and Klontz, P. T. (2023). *Psychology of Financial Planning: The Practitioner's Guide to Money and Behavior.* Hoboken, NJ: Wiley.

5. Klontz, B. T., and Britt, S. L. (2012). How clients' money scripts predict their financial behaviors. *Journal of Financial Planning, 25*(11), 33–43.

6. Britt, S. L., Klontz, B. T., Tibbetts, R., and Leitz, L. (2015). The financial health of mental health professionals. *Journal of Financial Therapy, 6*(1), 17–32.

7. Klontz, B. T., and Britt, S. L. (2012). Financial trauma: Why the abandonment of buy-and-hold in favor of tactical asset management may be a symptom of posttraumatic stress. *Journal of Financial Therapy, 3*(2), 14–27.

8. Ibid.

9. Klontz, B. T., Seay, M. C., Sullivan, P., and Canale, A. (2015). The wealthy: A financial psychological profile. *Consulting Psychology Journal: Practice and Research, 67*(2), 127–143.

10. Klontz, B. (2011). Behavioral modification: Clients may need your help discovering the childhood beliefs affecting their financial decisions today. *Financial Planning Magazine, 4.*

11. Klontz, B., Kahler, R., and Klontz, T. (2016). *Facilitating financial health: Tools for financial planners, coaches, and therapists,* 2nd edition. Cincinnati, OH: National Underwriters Company.

12. Klontz, B. T., Britt, S. L., Mentzer, J., and Klontz, T. (2011). Money beliefs and financial behaviors: Development of the Klontz Money Script Inventory. *Journal of Financial Therapy, 2*(1), 1–22.

13. Klontz, B. T., and Britt, S. L. (2012). How clients' money scripts predict their financial behaviors. *Journal of Financial Planning, 25*(11), 33–43.

14. Klontz, B., and Klontz, T. (2009). *Mind Over Money: Overcoming the Money Disorders That Threaten Our Financial Health.* New York, NY: Broadway Books.

15. Ibid.

Chapter 5

Financial Behaviors and Outcomes

Our financial behaviors are a result of our instincts, our financial flashpoint experiences, and our money scripts. Some financial behaviors have a positive impact on our financial health, while others make it difficult to achieve our financial goals. Through education and the use of communication and counseling techniques, financial planners can have a positive impact on shaping a client's money behaviors. Although they are not in the business of diagnosing or treating money disorders, it is important for financial planners to know what to look out for in the event that a client needs a referral to a mental health professional. What follows are two assessments that can be used with clients to examine their financial behaviors and outcomes.

Exercise 14: Financial Health Scale

Financial health is more than just net worth. It includes having a plan in place for the future to protect you and your family. Good financial health is having a sense of comfort and confidence around financial matters, low levels of financial stress, and good financial communication with your spouse/partner and family members. Conversely, poor financial health is associated with a host of physical and emotional problems, which is why it is a critical aspect of our overall well-being. According to the American Psychological Association's annual Stress in America™ survey, one of the top stressors in the lives of Americans is money.[1]

The following test has been used in measuring changes after a financial therapy intervention and is currently being used by many financial planners to take a quick snapshot of their clients' financial health.[2] It can be a useful assessment for measuring improvements in financial health as clients progress through the financial planning process. As such, it can be helpful to revisit this assessment three to six months after clients have had time to put things into action. A free online version of this test with an automatically generated custom report is available to the readers of this book at: http://www.bradklontz.com/financialhealthtest.

Financial Health Scale

Circle the number that best describes the extent that you agree or disagree with each of the following.

1 Strongly Disagree	2 Disa- gree	3 Disagree a Little	4 Agree a Little	5 Agree	6 Strongly Agree				
1. My spending is under control.					1	2	3	4	5	6
2. I understand my financial goals.					1	2	3	4	5	6
3. I am saving for my goals (e.g., school, car, house, etc.).					1	2	3	4	5	6
4. I have a spending budget.					1	2	3	4	5	6
5. I consistently follow my spending budget.					1	2	3	4	5	6
6. I have clear financial goals for the future.					1	2	3	4	5	6
7. Financial issues do not depress me.					1	2	3	4	5	6
8. I am proud of how I handle money.					1	2	3	4	5	6
9. I do not avoid thinking about money.					1	2	3	4	5	6
10. I rarely buy things in an attempt to make me feel better.					1	2	3	4	5	6
11. The way I manage money is consistent with my values, goals, and dreams.					1	2	3	4	5	6
12. I do obsess about financial matters.					1	2	3	4	5	6
13. I have money set aside for emergencies.					1	2	3	4	5	6
14. Financial issues do not confuse me.					1	2	3	4	5	6
15. I do not spend more money than I can afford to.					1	2	3	4	5	6
16. I do not have many fears or insecurities around money.					1	2	3	4	5	6

Psychology of Financial Planning: Practitioner's Toolkit

17. I am taking the steps necessary to meet my financial goals.	1	2	3	4	5	6
18. I do not have trouble controlling my impulse to buy things.	1	2	3	4	5	6
19. I do not let others take advantage of me financially.	1	2	3	4	5	6
20. I am comfortable talking about money issues.	1	2	3	4	5	6

Total score: _____

Scoring Instructions

Add up your total score. Scores on the financial health scale range from 20 to 100. The higher the financial health score, the better your financial health.

20–39: Poor Financial Health   It is likely that you are in a significant amount of pain in your relationship with money. You may lack clear financial goals, have difficulty saving, and your spending may be out of control. It is likely that you experience conflict in your relationships around money and it may also be a significant source of guilt, shame, depression, and confusion. Your financial behaviors do not correspond with your values. You may lack important financial information, and you would benefit from assistance in discovering and working through emotional blocks around money that are keeping you stuck.

40–59: At-Risk Financial Health   It is likely that you are experiencing some pain in your relationship with money. You may lack clear financial goals, have difficulty saving, and you may be spending in ways that are not consistent with your values. You may be experiencing some conflict in your relationships around money and you may have some difficult emotions related to finances, including guilt, shame, depression, or confusion. It is likely you would benefit from further financial education and possible assistance in discovering and working through emotional blocks around money that may be keeping you stuck.

60–79: Fair Financial Health   While there may be some positive aspects in your relationship with money, it is likely that you are not realizing your full emotional and financial potential. While not causing you overwhelming distress, your financial behaviors may not be fully consistent with your values and goals. Further financial education and possible assistance in exploring your historical relationship with money may help you better reach your financial goals, strengthen your relationships, and improve your emotional functioning related to money.

80–100: Good Financial Health It is likely that you have a relatively healthy relationship with money. You have clear financial goals, are taking steps to achieve your goals, and are effectively executing a savings and spending plan. You are likely open and honest with those close to you regarding financial issues and have found ways to successfully negotiate financial issues in your relationships.

Exercise 15: Klontz Money Behavior Inventory (KMBI)

The KMBI was designed as a quick measure of financial behaviors. It is not designed to "diagnose" a behavioral problem in clients, but rather, as a quick screener to flag potential concerns. The KMBI is an example of a psychology of financial planning tool that would not be used in the majority of financial planning engagements, and is best suited for financial planners who have been formally trained in the psychology of financial planning and the administration, scoring, and interpreting of the test. However, we have included it here for educational purposes and encourage our readers to take it to see the areas that are covered to help determine if and when such an assessment might be appropriate depending on their specialty and area of practice. A free online version of this test with an automatically generated custom report is available to the readers of this book at: https://www.bradklontz.com/moneybehaviortest.

Klontz Money Behavior Inventory (KMBI)

Please indicate how strongly you agree with the following statements using the following scale:

1 = Strongly Disagree, 2 = Disagree, 3 = Disagree a Little, 4 = Agree a Little, 5 = Agree, 6 = Strongly Agree

		1 **Strongly** **Disagree**	2 **Disagree**	3 **Disagree** **a Little**	4 **Agree** **a Little**	5 **Agree**	6 **Strong-** **ly** **Agree**
1.	My spend-ing feels out of control.						
2.	I obsess about shopping.						
3.	I buy more things than I need or can afford.						
4.	I feel irresistible urges to shop.						
5.	I shop to forget about my problems and make myself feel better.						
6.	I feel guilt and/or shame after making purchases.						
7.	I often return items because I feel bad about buying them.						

(continued)

Financial Behaviors and Outcomes

		1 **Strongly Disagree**	2 **Disagree**	3 **Disagree a Little**	4 **Agree a Little**	5 **Agree**	6 **Strongly Agree**
8.	I have tried to reduce my spending but have had trouble doing so.						
9.	I hide my spending from my partner/family.						
10.	I feel anxious or panicky if I am unable to shop.						
11.	Shopping interferes with my work or relationships.						
Signs of compulsive buying		**Sum =**		**Divided by 11**		**= Score:** _____	
12.	I have trouble controlling my gambling.						
13.	I gamble to relieve stress or make myself feel better.						

Psychology of Financial Planning: Practitioner's Toolkit

		1 **Strongly Disagree**	2 **Disagree**	3 **Disagree a Little**	4 **Agree a Little**	5 **Agree**	6 **Strong- ly Agree**
14.	I have to gamble with more and more money to keep it exciting.						
15.	I have committed an illegal act to get money for gambling.						
16.	I have borrowed money for gambling or have gambled on credit.						
17.	My gambling interferes with other aspects of my life (e.g., work, education, relationships).						
Signs of problematic gambling		**Sum =**		**Divided by 6**		**= Score:** _____	

(continued)

Financial Behaviors and Outcomes

		1 Strongly Disagree	2 Disagree	3 Disagree a Little	4 Agree a Little	5 Agree	6 Strong- ly Agree
18.	I have trouble throwing things away, even if they aren't worth much.						
19.	I feel irrespon- sible if I get rid of an item.						
20.	My living space is cluttered with things I don't use.						
21.	Throwing something away makes me feel like I am losing a part of myself.						
22.	I feel emotion- ally attached to my possessions.						
23.	My posses- sions give me a sense of safety and security.						

Psychology of Financial Planning: Practitioner's Toolkit

		1 Strongly Disagree	2 Disagree	3 Disagree a Little	4 Agree a Little	5 Agree	6 Strong- ly Agree
24.	I have trouble using my living space because of clutter.						
25.	I hide my need to hold onto items from others.						
Signs of hoarding		**Sum =**		**Divided by 13**		**= Score:**	
26.	I often feel an irresistible drive to work.						
27.	My family complains about how much I work.						
28.	I feel guilty when I take time off of work.						
29.	I feel a need to constantly stay busy.						

(continued)

		1 Strongly Disagree	2 Disagree	3 Disagree a Little	4 Agree a Little	5 Agree	6 Strongly Agree
30.	I often miss important family events because I am working.						
31.	I have trouble falling or staying asleep because I am thinking about work.						
32.	I have made promises to myself or others to work less but have had trouble keeping them.						
33.	It is hard for me to enjoy time off of work.						

Psychology of Financial Planning: Practitioner's Toolkit

		1 Strongly Disagree	2 Disagree	3 Disagree a Little	4 Agree a Little	5 Agree	6 Strong- ly Agree
34.	People close to me complain that I am so focused on my to-do lists that I ignore them or brush aside their needs or concerns.						
35.	I have trouble saying "no" when asked to work extra hours or take on extra projects.						
Signs of workaholism		**Sum =**		**Divided by 10**		**= Score:**	
36.	I feel like the money I get comes with strings attached.						
37.	I often feel resentment or anger related to the money I receive.						

(continued)

Financial Behaviors and Outcomes

		1 **Strongly Disagree**	2 **Disagree**	3 **Disagree a Little**	4 **Agree a Little**	5 **Agree**	6 **Strongly Agree**
38.	A significant portion of my income comes from money I do nothing to earn (e.g., trust fund, compensation payments).						
39.	I have significant fear or anxiety that I will be cut off from my nonwork income.						
40.	The nonwork income I receive seems to stifle my motivation, passion, creativity, and/or drive to succeed.						
Signs of financial dependence		**Sum =**		**Divided by 5**		**= Score:**	

Psychology of Financial Planning: Practitioner's Toolkit

		1 **Strongly Disagree**	2 **Disagree**	3 **Disagree a Little**	4 **Agree a Little**	5 **Agree**	6 **Strongly Agree**
41.	I give money to others even though I can't afford it.						
42.	I have trouble saying "no" to requests for money from family or friends.						
43.	I sacrifice my financial well-being for the sake of others.						
44.	People take advantage of me around money.						
45.	I lend money without making clear arrangements for repayment.						

(*continued*)

89

Financial Behaviors and Outcomes

		1 **Strongly Disagree**	2 **Disagree**	3 **Disagree a Little**	4 **Agree a Little**	5 **Agree**	6 **Strongly Agree**
46.	I often find myself feeling resentment or anger after giving money to others.						
Signs of financial enabling		Sum =		Divided by 6		= Score:	
47.	I avoid thinking about money.						
48.	I try to forget about my financial situation.						
49.	I avoid opening/looking at my bank statements.						
Signs of financial denial		Sum =		Divided by 3		= Score:	
50.	I feel better after I talk to my children (under 18) about my financial stress.						

Psychology of Financial Planning: Practitioner's Toolkit

		1 Strongly Disagree	2 Disagree	3 Disagree a Little	4 Agree a Little	5 Agree	6 Strong- ly Agree
51.	I talk to my children (under 18) about my financial stress.						
52.	I ask my children (under 18) to pass on financial messages to other adults.						
Signs of financial enmeshment		Sum =		Divided by 3		= Score:	

Scoring Key

- Scores lower than or equal to 3: Suggest you do not exhibit significant signs of the money behavior.
- Scores between 3 and 4: Suggest you exhibit some signs of the money behavior.
- Scores higher than 4: Suggest you exhibit many signs of the money behavior.

Exercise 16: Mindfulness Meditation

Often we act out financially, or in other ways, in response to a feeling of loneliness, isolation, or emptiness. Although temporary, financial behaviors can offer immediate relief or distraction, but their consequences compound our difficulties. In our financial therapy programs, we include daily mindfulness exercises.[3] The goals of these exercises are to enhance body awareness, reduce anxiety, and facilitate a feeling of connection and wholeness. Creating a sense of connection to self and/or a greater whole will decrease our temptation to fill a psychic or emotional hole with self-destructive financial behaviors.[4] It is important to note that mindfulness, essentially nonjudgmentally focusing on the present, has been found to have detrimental effects on our financial health, given that focusing on the rewards now is associated with investing less for the future.[5] However, most of our suffering comes from worrying about the future or regretting the past so there are a multitude of psychological benefits that can come from mindfulness.

Instructions

Set aside time in the coming days for three mindfulness meditation sessions. These sessions start at just five minutes. Here are several mindfulness exercises you can try.

1. Sitting meditation. Set an alarm for five minutes. Find a comfortable seat. Close your eyes. Focus on your breathing. You could count to 10 with each inhale and exhale and then start over, or repeat the words "in" as you inhale and "out" as you exhale. It doesn't really matter how you do it. As you are occupied with this activity, observe what is going on in your mind. At first there will likely be a jumble of thoughts and concerns. Don't try to fight them or push them away. Just observe them with curiosity, say to yourself, "Oh, there is a thought," let it go, then return to focusing on your breathing.

2. Eating meditation. The Vietnamese Buddhist monk and mindfulness meditation teacher Thich Nhat Hanh was once asked for his advice on how to lose weight. He said, "Eat half as much." The individual then asked, "Well, what do you do if you are still hungry?" He said, "Eat twice as slow." Mealtime is a great time to practice mindfulness, even if for just a few minutes. Instead of gulping down your food mindlessly while watching television, take some time to be present while you are eating. Take a bite of food and put your fork down. Chew it slowly, 30 times, before you swallow. Focus on the taste, the smell, and the texture of your food.

3. Fill-in-the-blank meditation. The great thing about mindfulness is that you can engage in the practice while you are doing other things. The key is to stay in the moment; to focus on the experience – the physical sensation, the sounds,

the smells, the sights. When your mind wanders, you simply note it and return your attention back to your experience. The following are just a few of the activities you can do mindfully. Even if you practice mindfulness for just a few seconds or minutes throughout the course of these activities, you will begin to notice benefits.

- Washing dishes
- Playing tennis
- Going for a walk
- Swimming
- Folding laundry
- Vacuuming
- Mowing the lawn
- Playing with a child

Notes

1. American Psychological Association. (2022). *Stress in America™ infographics: March 2022.* https://www.apa.org/news/press/releases/stress/2022/infographics-march
2. Klontz, B. T., Bivens, A., Klontz, P. T., Wada, J., and Kahler, R. (2008). The treatment of disordered money behaviors: Results of an open clinical trial. *Psychological Services*, 5(3), pp. 295–308.
3. Ibid.
4. Klontz, B., and Klontz, T. (2009). *Mind Over Money: Overcoming the Money Disorders That Threaten Our Financial Health*. New York, NY: Broadway Books.
5. Bazley, W., Cuculiza, C., and Pisciotta, K. (2021, October 24). *Being present: The influence of mindfulness on financial decisions*. Available at SSRN: https://ssrn.com/abstract=3921871 or http://dx.doi.org/10.2139/ssrn.3921871

Chapter 6

Principles of Effective Communication

Being an effective financial planner requires impactful and honest communication. Communication is more than just presenting a financial plan or speaking eloquently. It involves skills related to listening, nonverbal communication, and techniques to build trust and ensure that the client knows they are being heard. In this section, we focus on techniques that will help you build a deeper relationship with your client and ensure that you are effective in listening and responding to their goals and needs.

Open-Ended Invitations Versus Closed-Ended Questions

Closed-ended questions are efficient and can be great for gathering information. They typically prompt clients to give single-word or short-phrase responses. For example:

Advisor: *"Do you have a Will?"*
Client: *"Yes."*
Advisors: *"When do you want to retire?"*
Client: *"When I am 62."*

The problem with closed-ended questions is that they leave little room for establishing rapport, limit the amount of information the client shares with the planner, and provide little room for the client to elaborate, limiting the client's ability to engage in self-discovery.

In contrast, open-ended questions invite the client to offer a more detailed response to a specific question. "Open-ended" means that there is room for an expanded response and "invitation" is substituted for "question," based on the research that shows that using a question leads to a physiological stress response.[1] So financial planners who are wanting to increase client rapport, set a client at ease, and facilitate client self-discovery will opt for open-ended invitations.

For example:

Advisor: *"Tell me about your estate planning."*
Client: *"Well, we have a Will but I have been wondering whether or not we should have a Trust. Is that something you help clients figure out?"*
Advisor: *"Paint me a picture about your ideal retirement."*
Client: *"I would like to retire at 62 and spend more time with my partner. I would like to do some traveling and put more time into volunteer work. I'd also like to spend more time playing golf and pickleball."*

Exercise 17: Open-Ended Invitation

For this exercise, change these closed-ended questions to open-ended invitations.

Closed-ended question:	*"How much are you contributing to your retirement account each month?"*
Open-ended invitation:	_____
Closed-ended question:	*"Do you and your partner have similar financial goals?"*
Open-ended invitation:	_____
Close-ended question:	*"Do you plan on leaving your assets to your children?"*
Open-ended invitation:	_____

Reflection

Reflection is the act of verifying and clarifying what the client is conveying. This is a process where the advisor reflects back periodically what the client is saying; it serves multiple purposes:

- It ensures that the client knows they are being heard.
- It assists the financial planner in understanding what the client is saying.
- It helps the client gain clarity as they: (a) formulate their thoughts, (b) put them into words, (c) hear themselves say them, and then (d) hear the financial planner repeat them back to them.

Simple reflection is anything but simple. It is much more than just parroting back what a client says. When done well, it is specific and purposeful and can help motivate the client to take action. The financial planner must choose what to reflect back to the client, considering the following:

- Would it be most helpful to reflect back the emotions of the client or the content of what was said?
- If reflecting back the content of what was said, which parts of what the client said will be reflected and for what end?

Consider the following example: Steven is meeting with his financial planner Roberta to discuss his retirement planned for later this year. He begins talking about his hesitancy to retire and begin this new chapter.

Steven:	*"I am not sure I am ready to stop earning. I have worked all my life. I started with delivering newspapers when I was 13. I am going to now walk away from a high-paying job and hope that I have enough money? What if I run out? It is kind of terrifying. At the same time, I am sick of this job but I don't want my accounts to start dwindling."*
Roberta:	*"You have worked all your life and are worried that you are going to run out of money."*
Steven:	*"Yes. I can't go back to my job after I leave. Besides, when I run out of money, I will probably be too old to work anyway."*
Roberta:	*"You're also concerned that once you make this move, there is no turning back?"*
Steven:	*"Yes. And then what? . . . I mean, I guess I could do some consulting to try to ease my way into retirement."*
Roberta:	*"Consulting could give you something to continue some basic income and reduce some of your anxiety."*

In this vignette, Roberta worked to reflect the gravity of Steven's concern over running out of money in retirement. She also provided him the space to consider a short-term option (in this case, consulting) that could alleviate his concerns and help him transition a little more slowly into retirement.

Exercise 18: Reflection Exercise

Now it's your turn to do some reflecting:

During a meeting with her advisor, Jamie began discussing her concerns over her two children's current income and their ability to support their families.

Jamie: *"I wonder if I need to retire later than planned. I stay awake at night wondering if these kids are going to be able to make ends meet. How can they possibly make enough to live where they do and still provide a good life for a family of four? At the same time, I also worry that if I start supporting them, when does it stop? Could they become dependent on me to a point that they aren't ambitious enough in their careers to stand on their own two feet?"*

If you were her advisor, how would you use reflection to ensure that Jamie is feeling heard and that you fully understand her concerns? How would you address the internal conflict that Jamie is experiencing regarding helping her children financially? Choose three things you could reflect to Jamie as her advisor in the spaces below:

1. _____

2. _____

3. _____

Exercise 19: Question-Free Zone Exercise

Now that we have discussed what questions you should ask, we suggest that you don't ask any questions at all. Asking a question, such as a request for information, usually ends in an "upward" inflection of the voice. In written form, a request for information typically ends with a question mark. For example, let's take the question "How did you make that decision?" When said aloud, note the ascending inflection of your voice at the end. For many individuals, a question implies that there may be a "right/acceptable" or "wrong/unacceptable" answer. Our subconscious picks up on that "test." When a person is asked a question concerning sensitive information, such as their finances, it can create a stress response. Blood pressure, heart rate, sweat glands, respiration rates, and stress hormones respond as if experiencing a stress event. Increased stress levels negatively impact interpersonal relationships. It's not the request for information that creates the distress, it is the form that the request takes.

Posing the request in the form of a statement that ends with the voice inflection descending (if written, having the statement end in a period) has been shown to lower stress indicators. For example, "I'd like to know more about how you made that decision" is requesting the same information as if asked in question form, but the subconscious reacts differently. It is less likely to perceive that there is a right and wrong answer. It is more likely to experience it as someone desiring to know more out of curiosity.

With your clients or classmates, create a list of 20 questions you would normally ask them if you were meeting them for the first time. These questions will be general in nature, things you might normally ask someone you don't know well, such as where they were born, the kind of house they grew up in, whether they have siblings, if they have pets, and so on. If you are a practicing financial planner and have an intake questionnaire, feel free to use it for this exercise.

1. _____

2. _____

3. _____

4. _____

5. _____

6. _____

7. _____

8. _____

9. _____

10. _____

11. _____

12. _____

13. _____

14. _____

15. _____

16. _____

17. _____

18. _____

19. _____

20. _____

Now look at each question and turn each one into a statement. For example, "Did you grow up in the city or the country?" becomes "I'm wondering if you grew up in the city or the country." "Did you have any pets growing up?" becomes "Tell me about any pets you had growing up." Other "starter" phrases include:

- "I'm curious about . . ."
- "Tell me more about . . ."
- "Say more about . . ."
- "I would like to know about . . ."
- "I'd love to hear about. . ."

Take those 20 questions that you started with and convert each one of them into a statement.

1. _____

2. _____

3. _____

4. _____

5. _____

6. _____

7. _____

8. _____

9. _____

10. _____

11. _____

12. _____

13. _____

14. _____

15. _____

16. _____

17. _____

18. _____

19. _____

20. _____

Exercise 20: Dirty Dozen Exercise

Relationships fail all the time, and much of that failure has been attributed to a breakdown in communication. Dr. Thomas Gordon identified common roadblocks to effective communication.[2] These roadblocks have also been referred to as the "Dirty Dozen." At first glance you may wonder that if these communication approaches are all problematic, "What else is there if I am not supposed to use these tools?" We ask that you read through the following list with an open mind, as these communication strategies are deeply embedded in our culture's communication process.

Each of the following tools can be effective if used at the right time, in the right situation, and in the right amounts. However, there are often much more effective ways to communicate. For this exercise, watch a news show of your choice on which there is a panel of people with differing opinions speaking on the same topic. Some suggestions include, but are not limited to, CNN, Fox News, or MSNBC. As you watch the segment, track the communication strategies used. Any time you hear one of the "Dirty Dozen," make a tally mark next to the strategy below. Please also complete the section at the end of the list with the show details.

_____ 1. Ordering directly, commanding

_____ 2. Warning or threatening

_____ 3. Giving advice, suggestions, solutions

_____ 4. Persuading with logic

_____ 5. Moralizing

_____ 6. Judging, disagreeing, blaming

_____ 7. Agreeing, approving, praising

_____ 8. Shaming, ridiculing

_____ 9. Interpreting, analyzing

_____ 10. Reassuring, sympathizing, consoling

_____ 11. Questioning

_____ 12. Withdrawing, humoring, distracting

_____	_____
Name of Show	Date and Time

Exercise 21: The FLOW Process

The goal of this exercise is to practice listening so that you can see and understand someone else's perspective precisely as they see it.[3] FLOW in this case means following the flow, or energy, of the speaker. One of the most powerful communication tools is listening. Most people understand that interrupting someone would constitute "not listening." However, merely being quiet until the other person stops talking doesn't mean that listening is taking place.

Being in the presence of a skilled listener helps the speaker gain clarity about not only what they are trying to say but what they actually mean. Taking an abstract feeling or experience and trying to share it using words is terribly inefficient, so it takes some time to get to the point where the speaker says exactly what they are trying to communicate. Through the process of hearing themselves talk, many clients will gain additional insights, leading to their modifying or changing what they previously believed.

During this process, note those times you have the urge to comment or ask a question. Those are moments when you have stopped listening. It is also important to know that the moment you ask for more information about something a speaker has said, you have taken control of the narrative, which may not be helpful for the client. That is why we suggest that you ask for additional information as late in the listening process as you can. If you listen well, most of the things you would have wanted to ask about will have been answered by the speaker without you interrupting them.

1. Ask a friend, colleague, or classmate to talk about a time in their life when someone saw something in them that they couldn't quite see in themselves. Perhaps it was a coach who suggested that they try out for a team; a teacher who suggested that they apply for a scholarship; or a boss who suggested that they should "go for" a new position. Tell the speaker that you will be practicing some enhanced communication skills that you'll be happy to share after the two of you are done.

2. Once the speaker begins, you will stay silent, but at the same time letting the speaker know, nonverbally, that you are listening. This can be accomplished through periodic eye contact, head tilting, and head nodding. You will listen until:

a. You need to summarize to make room in your head for new information, or

b. You notice the speaker's energy sink/go down.

3. When either of those two things happen, you will then summarize what you have heard, in no more than three concise sentences, capturing the essence of what the speaker has said. It is better to choose a theme than a specific sentence. The speaker may interrupt you at any point during your summary and, if they do, let that happen and continue to listen as noted in step 2.

4. If that doesn't increase the energy, ask for more information about something that the speaker has said.

5. Repeat steps 2 and 3 several times.

6. When the speaker is finished, construct a grand summary of three sentences or less.

7. Ask the speaker to tell you what you might have missed. If they mention that you missed something, make sure to summarize that final thing. *Note:* This missed piece of information is often one of the most important things the individual has shared with you.

When practicing the FLOW process, it can be helpful to have these steps listed and in front of you. As you gain experience, you will no longer need to refer to these steps during the conversation and you will integrate the concept into your conversational repertoire.

Exercise 22: Listening by Sketch

This listening strategy could be used with clients but could also be adapted to use with anyone (colleague, spouse, partner, friend, etc.). Ask a friend, colleague, or classmate if they would be willing to let you practice some enhanced communication skills with them. Ask if they would be willing to talk about their ideal retirement.

Tell them that you will listen without saying anything for two minutes. At the end of the two minutes, take a pencil and paper and sketch or create an image that would represent what you have heard them say. You can either take a few moments to draw after they are done speaking or share the sketch as you are drawing it. It doesn't really matter what the picture looks like. Artistic ability is irrelevant for this exercise. The drawing is a visual analogy. Its purpose is to give the speaker something to react to with the goal of helping them define their thoughts more clearly and help you gather more information. The simple act of attempting to sketch will have a valuable effect.

Allow the speaker to correct and/or adjust. When using this technique with clients, they will sometimes respond to the drawing with "That's it exactly" or "That's not it at all." In the case of the latter, you can simply say, "Show me what it does look like." In either case, you will learn more about what the client is saying, and the client will gain clarity about identifying their most salient concerns.

Notes

1. Miller, W. and Rollnick, S. (2022). *Motivational Interviewing: Helping People Change* (third ed.). New York, NY: Guilford Press.
2. Gordon, T. (2000). *Parent Effectiveness Training: The Proven Program for Raising Responsible Children*. New York, NY: Three Rivers Press.
3. Klontz, B. T., and Klontz, P. T. (2016). 7 steps to facilitate exquisite listening. *Journal of Financial Planning*, 29(11), pp. 24–26.

Chapter 7

Client and Planner Attitudes, Values, and Biases

Client meetings involve learning. In some cases, it is the client learning about ways to meet their goals, and in others, it is part of a process where the client learns about themselves and what drives them in their work and personal lives. Regardless, learning is taking place. We all learn in a variety of ways and the more effective the financial planner is at understanding the learning style of their client, the more effective their meetings will be.

The Six Main Learning Styles

1. Visual

Visual learners prefer charts, graphics, maps, images, colors, and maps to receive and communicate information and ideas. Some signs that a person may be a visual learner include:

- Their thoughts wander during verbal conversations.
- They are visually observant, but they miss things that are said verbally.
- They enjoy reading and intensely focus while reading.
- They find charts, graphs, and diagrams helpful in remembering information.
- They desire *seeing* directions rather than *hearing* them.

2. Auditory

Auditory learners prefer to receive information through listening and hearing. Some signs that a person is an auditory learner include:

- They like to talk.
- They prefer spoken directions to written directions.
- They prefer audio books to reading.

3. Reading/Writing

Some clients prefer to learn information by reading notes, handouts, or textbooks. Reading/writing learners also benefit by rewriting notes and rereading those notes silently again and again. Some signs that a person learns best from reading/writing include:

- They prefer to review materials ahead of time.
- They write a lot.
- They tend to review their planner's advice on the web and compare.

4. Logical

Logical learners prefer to use reason and logic to process information. Some signs of a logical preferred learning style include:

- They learn through inquiry.
- They interrupt at times with questions or to complete the planner's sentence.

5. Kinesthetic

Kinesthetic learners prefer physical activity while they are taking in new ideas and information. Some signs of a kinesthetic learner include:

- They enjoy movement.
- They tend to fidget.
- They pace while they are talking on the phone.

6. Social Versus Solitary Learners

Social learners may want to learn from a group or discuss things with others before they make decisions. In contrast, a solitary learner may want to discuss financial options privately with their spouse so they can process the information on their own.

A Multifaceted Approach

When in doubt, mix it up. One of the best ways to begin to understand the learning style of your client is to start with a mix of approaches, including auditory, visual, and ways that kinesthetic and logical learners can engage throughout your meeting. You can then begin to see what approach is resonating the most with your client and adjust for future meetings. In many cases, individuals prefer a hybrid approach.

Exercise 23: Learning Style Exercise

How well are you accommodating the different learning styles of your current (or future) clientele? Circle your answer to the following questions:

- Do you have a sense of the learning style(s) of each of your clients? Yes or No
- Do you accommodate visual learners with charts and graphs and verbal discussion that supports the images? Yes or No
- Do you routinely check in with your clients for understanding when you are presenting information regarding their financial plan? Yes or No
- Do you have items that your clients can use to take notes and/or fidget with in your office? Yes or No

Client and Planner Attitudes, Values, and Biases

- In your initial conversations with a client, do you prepare for multiple learning styles? Yes or No

- Do you ask your clients their preferred learning style at the beginning of your relationship? Yes or No

Active Versus Passive

No matter how many years of experience we have working with clients, we should pay attention to how much we are talking versus listening. It is important to make the distinction between talking *with* someone and talking *at* them. A useful guideline for planners is the seven-minute rule. A planner should not keep talking in a client presentation for more than seven minutes at a time before pausing and checking in with the client and inviting responses, discussion, or feedback. If a planner is presenting something complex or stressful, seven minutes might be too much. The more complex or stressful a topic, the less time should go by before a planner checks in to make sure the client is comfortable with and is following the presentation. Our conversations and presentations are a partnership with our clients, requiring us to act as facilitators relative to client learning and action toward reaching their financial goals.

Exercise 24: The 75% Rule

A helpful approach when it comes to client conversations is to employ the 75% rule, where you listen 75% of the time and spend just 25% of the time talking. Reflect on your most recent client conversation and estimate the percentage of time you spent listening during the interaction. If you spent most of the time talking, how could you use one or more of the communication techniques discussed earlier to listen more? In your next conversation and/or client meeting, try to spend 75% of your time listening and just 25% of the time talking, and then reflect on the following:

- How did the conversation go?

_____

_____

_____

_____

_____

_____

_____

_____

_____

_____

- Did it feel the same or different from previous conversations?

_____

_____

_____

_____

_____

_____

_____

_____

_____

_____

- How do you think the other person experienced the conversation?

_____

_____

_____

_____

_____

_____

_____

_____

_____

_____

Attention

Attention is the gateway to consciousness. Every experience, whether working, learning, conversing, or processing, starts with our attention. In other words, if our attention is not focused, we will have little chance of meeting our goals. Therefore, within every client meeting, our focused attention is necessary in order to listen, respond, and ultimately build strong and trusting relationships with our clients.

Exercise 25: The Distraction Checklist

Look around your workplace. Whether you have client meetings in your office or via video conference, note all of the items that might be distracting to you. They could be:

- Your smartphone
  - How are you handling push notifications? Are they off?
  - Where do you store your phone when you are working or in meetings? Just putting it face down still can be distracting, even when it is turned off.
- Your computer/laptop
  - How are you handling your email inbox? Is the mailbox open and alerting you every time you get a message?

- Do you keep multiple unnecessary windows open simultaneously?
- Is your screen a distraction when you are meeting with a client?
- Your workspace
  - Do you have a television within your field of vision?
  - Is there background music or news playing in your workspace?
  - Is it an open office space and are you facing a coworker continuously?
- Other items that might be distracting you
  - What can you do to minimize your distraction?

Exercise 26: The Client Distraction Checklist

Let's now think through things that could be distracting your clients. Refer to the items above and consider whether they could also be distracting to your clients during meetings. If something is stealing your attention, there is a decent chance it is also stealing your client's attention if they are meeting with you in the same space. Make a note of the items below and consider altering the environment to decrease distractions.

_____

_____

_____

_____

_____

_____

_____

_____

_____

Client and Planner Attitudes, Values, and Biases

Chapter 8

Sources of Money Conflict: Working with Couples and Families

Money is often a source of conflict in relationships. In fact, it is quite uncommon to have a couple agree on every aspect of their financial lives. When relationships are strained by money conflicts, it can have a negative impact on a client's financial and emotional well-being and on the quality and longevity of the relationship. In their extreme, conflicts around money can threaten relationships and have a negative impact on a client's financial health. When partners have conflicting money scripts, financial conflict is inevitable.

Since money is a relatively taboo topic in our culture, many couples are married before they find out how different their individual financial beliefs, behaviors, and goals may be. Around the time they are sharing their goals for the future – career goals, family planning goals, and so on – couples should be having discussions about their financial values and goals. However, many couples neglect this topic of discussion, often because they haven't put much thought into it individually. However, each partner is coming into the relationship with their history around money and their own assumptions, values, and goals. In many cases opposites attract, perhaps in the partners' attempt to create a sense of balance around money or to heal certain parts of themselves. For example, an anxious saver might be attracted to a partner who is more fun-loving, or a person who is great at enjoying today may be attracted to someone who is good at planning for the future. While these different approaches to money can be quite complementary, they can also be a source of disagreements and resentments that build up over time.

Financial conflict between newlyweds can actually predict divorce.[1] Financial issues can be a primary focus of conflict for a couple. When a planner meets with a couple, they are also engaging all of their unresolved issues from their past. Resolving those past issues is essential if the couple is hoping to meet their financial goals. Sometimes, compromise is the best outcome from a couple so they can get beyond their unresolved differences and move forward. Changing one another is not usually an option so it is best for each member of the couple to recognize their individual differences with empathy and concern. For example, if one partner has a strong desire to give to others, it may make sense for the couple to agree to set aside a certain amount of money for the giver to donate to charity, which can satisfy their desire to donate while also taking their financial goals into consideration.

Money conflicts are essentially conflicting money scripts, since each individual has their own past experiences, family history, careers, and interpretations of events. An ideal destination for a couple is to examine their own money scripts, as well as each other's, so they can move toward understanding and empathy. It is there that some form of resolution is possible.

Exercise 27: Conversation Intervention

Money is a top source of stress in the lives of Americans, and one of the most common sources of conflict for couples. Most money conversations between couples occur clumsily, where throughout the course of the day, one or both partners will bring up money concerns in passing: a sarcastic comment here, a frustrated remark there. These types of money conversations rarely solve anything. In fact, they make matters worse, leaving the partners feeling resentful, disrespected, and misunderstood.

In our work with couples, the Conversation Intervention has helped couples have a different conversation around money, setting the stage for increased empathy and an enhanced ability to negotiate solutions to money conflicts that were previously at an impasse. This intervention can be used for couples, or adapted for use with business partners, family members, and/or friends. A financial planner might facilitate this conversation directly with the clients or give it as a homework assignment for them to do in between meetings. It is meant to lay the groundwork for conflict resolution by providing a structure to facilitate deeper understanding of oneself and one's partner and their psychology around money.

Instructions

What follows are six instructions for having a conversation about money with a spouse, partner, business partner, family member, or friend. In fact, these instructions are useful for conversations around any potentially emotionally charged topic.

1. **Set an appointment.** Agree not to engage in "drive-by" money conversations. Set a time and place to talk. Show up ready to listen. Your readiness to listen can be enhanced by taking a few moments to breathe deeply and set aside the stress of the day.

2. **Sit "knees-to-knees."** Set up two chairs facing each other with nothing in between. Sit with your knees anywhere from a few inches to a few feet away from your partner, according to your comfort level.

3. **Pick a speaker and a listener.**

4. **Use reflective listening.** The speaker talks for one to two minutes. The listener listens, then summarizes what they have heard, without analyzing, interpreting, asking questions, or arguing. This is a very challenging task for most people, especially when the issue is a hot topic and/or the couple has had a history of conflict around the topic. The listener reflects back what they think was said. The speaker then says: (a) "yes, that's it" or (b) clarifies. If the speaker offers a clarification, the listener reflects back what was said.

5. **Switch roles and repeat as needed.** For this exercise, each person can take turns sharing their answer to each question in turn.

6. **Take time out.** Emotional flooding is poison to a relationship. When we are flooded, our thinking brain goes offline and we end up doing or saying something we regret. If your anger or frustration reaches a level 6 on a scale of 1 to 10, take a 10- to 20-minute timeout, during which you both examine your role in where the conversation went bad. Then come back together and start again.

Sources of Money Conflict: Working with Couples and Families

Questions to Discuss

What follows are questions designed to facilitate a different type of money conversation. In our work with couples who are in conflict with money, we have found this intervention to help "soften" the often rigid and exaggerated defensive postures and stances people take when they feel misunderstood. Take time to reflect on these questions. This can be done in the moment as you are conversing or by taking some quiet time to reflect and journal in the days or hours before the conversation.

1. What is your earliest money memory?

_____

_____

_____

_____

_____

_____

_____

_____

_____

_____

2. What is your most joyful money memory?

_____

_____

_____

_____

_____

_____

_____

_____

_____

_____

3. What is your most painful memory of money?

_____

_____

_____

_____

_____

_____

_____

_____

_____

_____

4. What was the socioeconomic status of your family of origin? How did this impact your relationship with money?

_____

_____

_____

_____

Sources of Money Conflict: Working with Couples and Families

_____

_____

_____

_____

_____

_____

5. What was the original socioeconomic status of your parents? How do you think this impacted their relationship(s) with money?

_____

_____

_____

_____

_____

_____

_____

_____

_____

_____

6. Name three things you learned from your mother about money, either directly or indirectly.

_____

_____

_____

_____

_____

_____

_____

_____

_____

_____

7. Name three things you learned from your father about money, either directly or indirectly.

_____

_____

_____

_____

_____

_____

_____

_____

_____

_____

8. What are your financial goals?

_____

_____

_____

_____

_____

_____

_____

_____

_____

_____

_____

9. What are your biggest financial fears?

_____

_____

_____

_____

_____

_____

_____

_____

_____

_____

10. Name one or more things you are willing to do differently to improve your relationship.

_____

_____

_____

_____

_____

_____

_____

_____

_____

_____

11. List three values that you would like to guide your family's life.

_____

_____

_____

_____

_____

_____

_____

_____

_____

_____

12. Name three things you appreciate and admire about your partner.

_____

_____

_____

_____

_____

_____

_____

_____

_____

_____

Exercise 28: The Conversation for Blended Families

Money conflicts can become more complex when more than one family system is involved. Approximately 50% of Americans have lived or will live in a blended family situation at some point in their lives,[2] where one or both partners have children or stepchildren from previous relationships. Blended families face a common set of financial planning issues, and good communication can be a key factor in resilience. Van Cleve and Klontz (2022) have adapted the Conversation Intervention for use by financial planners working with blended families.[3] It uses the same instructions as previously but with a set of questions designed specifically for blended families.

Questions to Discuss

1. What is your earliest money memory?

_____

_____

_____

_____

_____

_____

_____

_____

_____

_____

2. What is your most joyful money memory?

_____

_____

_____

_____

_____

_____

_____

_____

_____

_____

3. What is your most painful memory of money?

_____

_____

_____

_____

_____

_____

_____

Sources of Money Conflict: Working with Couples and Families

_____

_____

_____

4. How have your prior marriage(s) and former relationships impacted your thoughts and feelings about money?

_____

_____

_____

_____

_____

_____

_____

_____

_____

5. Name three money mistakes from your prior relationship(s) that you want to avoid repeating.

_____

_____

_____

_____

_____

6. Name three positive money outcomes from your prior relationship(s) that you would like to continue.

_____

_____

_____

_____

_____

_____

_____

_____

_____

_____

7. What has been the most painful part of blending your family?

_____

_____

_____

_____

_____

_____

_____

_____

_____

_____

8. What has been the most enjoyable part of blending your family?

_____

_____

_____

_____

_____

_____

_____

_____

_____

_____

9. What are your estate planning goals?

_____

_____

_____

_____

_____

_____

_____

_____

_____

_____

10. How important is leaving a legacy for your biological kids? Stepchildren?

_____

_____

_____

_____

_____

_____

_____

_____

_____

_____

11. What are your biggest estate planning fears?

_____

_____

_____

_____

_____

_____

_____

_____

_____

_____

12. Name one or more things you are willing to do differently around money to improve your current relationship.

_____

_____

_____

_____

_____

_____

_____

_____

_____

13. List three values that you would like to guide your family's life.

_____

_____

_____

_____

_____

_____

_____

_____

_____

_____

14. Name three things you appreciate and admire about your partner.

_____

_____

_____

_____

_____

_____

_____

_____

_____

_____

_____

The Self-Aware Financial Planner

Working with couples and/or families in conflict comes with a unique set of challenges for the financial planner. To be most effective a financial planner needs to maintain a neutral stance. This can be quite challenging to do, as many people in conflict will attempt to get the advisor to take their side over the other person's side.

In some cases one or more of the individuals are looking for a financial planner to be the referee and tie-breaker in an ongoing dispute about what should or shouldn't be done. The same thing often happens with couples seeking couples therapy. Often one or both believe that they are "right" and the other person is "wrong" and want a third-party expert to support their belief. The problem with this approach, of course, is that both members of the relationship are likely contributing to the problem, and what looks like an extreme behavior is often taking place in a context that has been created and is being influenced by them both. In addition to potentially ignoring the context from which this dispute emerged and the dynamics of the couple, taking a side will alienate the "loser" in the debate and will very likely turn them off to financial planning. So even if an advisor feels like they took the "right" side of the conflict, have they really helped if one member of the couple or family has now fired them? As such, it is critical for a financial planner to remain neutral in their work with couples and families. This requires a planner to know themselves very well, which is easier said than done.

This is why it is important for financial planners to understand their own financial psychology. Having an intimate knowledge of your own financial flashpoints, biases, assumptions, and money scripts will help protect you from being sucked into a family drama and/or taking a side in a money conflict based on your own unresolved money issues. In psychological terms this is referred to as "countertransference."[4] Financial planners can minimize the potential negative impacts of their own countertransference by understanding their own emotional triggers, money scripts, and financial flashpoints.

In working with couples and families it can be helpful to think through one's own beliefs about how money should be done and one's own preferences around spending, saving, investing, and so on. With this in mind, take some time to reflect on the following questions:

1. How was money handled in your family?

_____

_____

_____

_____

_____

_____

_____

_____

_____

_____

2. How did you feel about how money was handled in your family?

_____

_____

_____

_____

_____

_____

_____

_____

_____

_____

3. How did your caregivers differ in their approaches to money?

_____

_____

_____

Sources of Money Conflict: Working with Couples and Families

_____

_____

_____

_____

_____

_____

_____

4. Which approach do you most identify with?

_____

_____

_____

_____

_____

_____

_____

_____

_____

_____

5. Do you believe that one of your caregivers was "right" and one was "wrong" when it came to certain money decisions?

_____

_____

_____

_____

_____

_____

_____

_____

_____

6. What are your opinions about how couples should approach money, including managing the household finances?

_____

_____

_____

_____

_____

_____

_____

_____

_____

_____

7. What are your opinions about whether couples "should" have joint accounts or separate accounts? *Note:* Are you aware that there are many couples who handle money differently than you think they "should" and are quite happy and financially healthy?

_____

_____

_____

_____

_____

_____

_____

_____

_____

8. What are your opinions about gender roles and money? Do you believe that one gender should do things in a certain way versus another?

_____

_____

_____

_____

_____

_____

_____

_____

_____

_____

9. What is your opinion on giving to charity or tithing?

_____

_____

_____

_____

_____

_____

_____

_____

_____

10. What does an ideal financial life look like for you? Your partner?

_____

_____

_____

_____

_____

_____

_____

Sources of Money Conflict: Working with Couples and Families

_____

_____

_____

Our primary job as financial planners is to be effective in our work with clients, not to be "right." Often, rigid stances held by clients begin to soften when a financial planner takes the time to truly understand the individual's perspective. As with all work with couples and families in other professions such as psychotherapy, financial planners will inevitably have stronger negative or positive emotions directed toward some individuals over others. This cannot be avoided. Instead, with a solid grasp of our own financial psychology and triggers, our job is to be aware of them when they arise, and to connect them to our own histories and potentially unresolved money conflicts, so that we can do our best to let them go in the moment and maintain a neutral and effective stance in our work with couples and families in money conflict.

Notes

1. Dew, J., Britt, S., and Huston, S. (2012). Examining the relationship between financial issues and divorce. _Family Relations_, 61, pp. 615–628.
2. Oppenheimer & Co., Inc. (2021, April 7.) _Wealth management: Estate planning for blended families._ www.oppenheimer.com/news-media/2021/insight/april/estate-planning-for-blended-families-print.aspx.
3. Van Cleve, M., and Klontz, B. (2022). The psychology of estate planning with blended families: How financial planners can better help blended families develop an estate plan that works. _Journal of Financial Planning_, 35(8), pp. 90–104.
4. Klontz, B., Kahler, R., and Klontz, T. (2016). _Facilitating Financial Health Tools for Financial Planners, Coaches, and Therapists_ (2nd ed.). National Underwriter Company.

Chapter 9

Helping Clients Navigate Crisis Events

Financial planners are intimately involved in the most important aspects of their clients' lives. Inevitably, clients will be forced to face crisis events, which we define as "an event that the client experiences as extremely difficult, emotionally troubling, or potentially dangerous."[1] That makes the role of the financial planner critically important in the lives of their clients as they help them navigate loss (e.g., the death of a loved one), transition from divorce or separation, or cope with natural disasters, diminished capacity, or a host of other expected and unexpected life events. While not therapists, financial planners are in an important position to not only help the client manage the financial aspects of a crisis event, but to be a source of emotional support and help them feel less isolated and alone.

The Financial Planner's Role in Helping a Client Navigate Crisis

In *Psychology of Financial Planning* we introduced a six-step model financial planners can use to help a client navigate a crisis event. The model was based on some of the core tenants of the Critical Incident Stress Debriefing (CISD) process.[2] CISD is not a form of psychotherapy, but rather an approach that helps a client return to normal functioning. As always, if a client is experiencing significant distress and/or having difficulty managing their lives, a referral to a mental health professional is highly recommended. However, it is possible that the planner may be the only professional to work with a client, and as such, having a model for working with clients in crisis is important. What follows is a deep dive into the six-step model for a financial planning crisis event, taken from the *Psychology of Financial Planning.*

Step 1: Normalize the Client's Experience

When a client is in crisis they likely feel overwhelmed. They may question how they are handling the situation or worry that others may see them as overreacting. Financial planners can help clients in crisis by taking a nonjudgmental stance, offering emotional support, and normalizing their experience. It can be helpful to remind the client that any information they share will be entirely confidential. To show support and help normalize the client's experiences, a financial planner might say one or more of the following:

"I am so sorry you are going through this."

"This is such a difficult thing."

"Of course you are feeling overwhelmed."

"There is no 'right' way to approach this."

"I don't know how you are feeling right now but I'm here to help."

"It is normal for people going through something like this to . . .

   . . . feel that way."

   . . . second-guess themselves."

Step 2: Encourage the Client to Talk About the Facts

In this step the financial planner encourages the client to recount the facts surrounding the incident in broad terms, without going into excessive detail.[3] This will help get the client talking without jumping too quickly into their thoughts and feelings about what is happening. It will help the client feel safe and maintain emotional control to give them time to feel more comfortable talking. This step is designed to help reduce anxiety and help the client maintain a sense of control around the conversation.[4] The following prompts are designed to help gather the facts around the situation.

"When did this happen?"

"How did you hear about it?"

"What did you do?"

"Where were you at the time of the event?"

"What happened?"

"What happened next?"

Step 3: Ask About the Client's Thought Process

In Step 3 the financial planner shifts the conversation from gathering facts to exploring the client's thoughts about what happened. This step is designed to be a gentle transition from facts to the client's experience of the crisis event without yet jumping into the emotionally triggering parts.[5] In this phase, a financial planner may ask the client one or more questions to explore their thoughts about the crisis event, such as:

"What went through your mind when you first found out?"
"What were your initial thoughts about what happened?"
"What have you been thinking about since the event?"

Step 4: Ask About the Client's Emotions and Reactions

Step 4 provides an opportunity for the client to share the emotional impact the event has had on them. Emotions like sadness, anger, confusion, frustration, loss, and other reactions may come out during this phase.[6] This is where utilizing communication techniques such as active listening is so important. Based on their comfort level, a client might express some feelings at this stage, such as crying or showing frustration. The financial planner's role is to just listen and NOT try to give advice or suggestions. Merely talking about one's emotional experience around a crisis event can be very therapeutic for a client. In Stage 4 a financial planner could ask one or more of the following:

"What was your immediate reaction?"
"How have you been feeling about what happened since?"
"What has been the hardest part of this for you?"

Step 5: Watch for Signs That the Client May Need Additional Support

Step 5 focuses on the effects of the event on the client's ability to cope with the situation.[7] The financial planner should be on the lookout for signs that the situation may be causing the client problems in their day-to-day functioning, such as high levels of stress, problems sleeping, or trouble concentrating at work. It is also important to check to make sure the client has adequate levels of social support to help them get through the period of crisis. If the financial planner notices that the client is having significant difficulty performing their various roles and duties, it is important that they make the case to the client that the client might benefit from the help of a mental health provider. Questions a financial planner might explore with the client in this phase include:

"Do you have people you can talk to about this?"

"Do you have the help you need to manage this?"

"Have you noticed anything that is different about yourself after this happened?"

"How have you been doing in other areas of your life since this happened?"

"Do you think you could benefit from some additional emotional support?"

Step 6: Modify the Financial Plan to Address the Crisis Event

In Step 6 the financial planner turns their focus to problem-solving. It might be necessary to revisit the financial plan and make changes based on the crisis event. If it looks like the client needs some additional emotional support, the financial planner might recommend that the client engage the services of a mental health provider. In addition to presenting the client with recommended changes to the financial plan identified by the financial planner, questions a financial planner might ask at this phase include:

"How do you think this event impacts your financial plan?"

"Are there any changes you are ready to make at this point?"

"Would you be open to a referral to someone who has experience in helping people navigate the emotional aspects of a crisis event like this?"

Notes

1. Klontz, B. T., Chaffin, C., and Klontz, P. T. (2023). *Psychology of Financial Planning: The Practitioner's Guide to Money and Behavior*. Hoboken, NJ: Wiley.
2. Mitchell, J. T. (n.d). *Critical Incident Stress Debriefing (CISD)*. info-trauma, Douglas Mental Health University and McGill University. http://www.info-trauma.org/flash/media-f/mitchell CriticalIncidentStressDebriefing.pdf (retrieved July 30, 2022).
3. Ibid.
4. Ibid.
5. Ibid.
6. Ibid.
7. Ibid.

Chapter 10

Principles of Counseling in Financial Planning Practice

A solid foundation in communication skills is essential for financial planners. Additionally, some basic principles and tools from counseling and psychology can be useful in establishing meaningful and trusting relationships with clients. Several of these techniques have been integrated into financial planning. In *Psychology of Financial Planning*, we introduced counseling approaches such as solution-focused, cognitive behavioral, positive psychology, and motivational interviewing. In this chapter, we offer some tools and techniques planners can use with clients that are drawn from solution-focused therapy (SFT), cognitive behavioral therapy (CBT), and positive psychology.

Solution-Focused Techniques in Financial Planning

One of the hallmark techniques in SFT is the miracle question. It is designed to help create an image of what someone would want their life to look like if a "miracle" occurred overnight and they woke up the next day with all of their problems solved and all of their goals met. After the client paints the picture of what their life would look like, the planner can ask follow-up questions to help them understand the positive changes the miracle would make in the client's life.[1] What follows is an example of the miracle question with some possible follow-up questions.

Exercise 29: The Miracle Question

As with all counseling techniques, it is helpful for a financial planner to go through the experience themselves before using it with a client. So take this opportunity to answer these questions yourself.

Tonight, while you're sleeping, a miracle happens and your biggest financial concerns are now solved. What would be the first signs you would notice in your life? What would other people notice? How would your thinking change? What would you be doing differently? How would it feel?

Follow-up questions could include one or more of the following:[2,3]

"How would you know that the miracle occurred?"

"What is the first thing you notice after the miracle occurs?"

"How do you know that things are different?"

"What would you be doing differently with your finances?"

"How would you know things are improving?"

"What would your family and friends notice about the differences in your life?"

"How would your feelings be different around your financial life?"

"What else would be different?"

"How would those changes make a difference in your life?"

"How might others act differently because of the changes?"

Cognitive Behavioral Techniques in Financial Planning

CBT assumes that our thoughts, feelings, physiology, and behavior are interconnected. It asserts that what happens to us shapes our thoughts, those thoughts affect our emotions, and those emotions drive our behaviors. The concept of money scripts, the Money Script Log (presented in chapter 4) and the cognitive reframing exercise New Money Mantra (presented in chapter 4) are all built on a CBT model. What follows is an additional CBT-influenced model that can help inoculate a client against anxiety related to their worst financial fears.

Exercise 30: Stress Inoculation: The Worst-Case Scenario

One of the tenets of CBT is that anxiety is made worse by avoidance and to reduce anxiety it can be helpful to expose oneself to the source of the anxiety. Rather than dismissing fears as being invalid it can be helpful to talk about the fear in detail. Crisis events and periods of unhappiness are a normal part of life. In fact, some experts suggest that the assumption that life should be free of challenges and that our normal or ideal state is one of "happiness" is a problem in and of itself. Happiness is overrated, and much of our suffering is related to our pursuit of happiness.[4] Often this pursuit is based on reaching a happiness goal—moving to a new place, making enough money, finding the right partner, publishing a book, having children, and so forth. Since a problem-free life of utopian happiness is unattainable, it is unreachable. So in the end we experience unhappiness when we reach our goals and unhappiness when we don't reach them. Recent research has shown that true happiness is only attained by accepting our unhappiness. It turns out that acceptance is a very important prerequisite for change.

Happiness is not a destination. It is not a goal. It is a state of mind, to which we all have immediate access. We can experience overwhelming joy when we bring our attention to the wonder of the moment. The key is to immerse ourselves in the experience of life—the wonderful taste of a cup of coffee in the morning, the incredible warmth of a hug from someone we love, focusing on feelings of gratitude for all we have in this moment, and so forth.

This exercise can be completed through a discussion with a client or as a journaling exercise.

1. What are your greatest financial fears?
2. Assuming that your greatest financial fears are realized, what is the worst thing you can picture happening?

For example:

- What would you lose?
- How would it impact your living situation?
- How would it impact the people you love most?
- How would it impact your self-concept?

- How would it impact your emotions?

- How would it impact your quality of life?

- How would it impact your goals?

3. Follow the worst-case scenario down as far as it can go. For example, if your fear is that you would lose your job, ask yourself: "Then what would happen?" At this stage DO NOT look for solutions; instead, dive deeper into the most likely worst-case scenario. For example, if you lost your job, the question "Then what would happen?" could lead to a statement such as "I would lose my house." Keep answering the question "Then what would happen?" and follow the most likely worst-case scenario spiral all the way down.

4. Prepare to accept these most dire consequences as if you have no choice. Then answer the following questions:

- What would you do?

- Where would you live?

- How would you get your needs met?

- How could you handle it cognitively (e.g., what would you say to yourself?)

- How could you handle it emotionally (e.g., how would you cope with or manage your feelings)?

5. Assuming the most likely worst-case scenario above, identify 10 things for which you would still be entirely grateful for having in your life.

1. _____

2. _____

3. _____

4. _____

5. _____

6. _____

7. _____

8. _____

9. _____

10. _____

6. Now that you have accepted the most likely worst consequences, what could you do to improve on the worst of these outcomes?

- What could you do to improve your situation?

- Assuming you made progress on improving, where would you see yourself in 5 years? In 10 years?

- What might you have learned from this experience? How might it have helped you?

Positive Psychology in Financial Planning

Positive psychology explores avenues to help people live fulfilling lives, and includes many areas of importance to financial planning, including: well-being, happiness, goal setting, gratitude, altruism, pursuit of meaningfulness, social support, and relationship connection.[5] Exercises from positive psychology have been proposed for use in a financial planning context by researchers, including the Gratitude Exercise (Exercise 35) and the Three Good Things Exercise (Exercise 36).[6]

Exercise 31: The Gratitude Exercise

Gratitude is a positive emotion that we feel when we consider the positive impact others have had on our lives. The Gratitude Exercise is a positive psychology technique that encourages clients to express gratitude to someone who has had a positive impact on lives in a meaningful way.[7] This exercise can be used in several ways in a financial planning context:

- It can be presented as described below in a workshop or client seminar-type setting.

Principles of Counseling in Financial Planning Practice

- As described below with clients who are seeking a financial planning experience that incorporates such self-discovery exercise.
- When working with multiple generations within a family or family business or non-family business to strengthen family relationships.
- Adapted to be just conversational in nature, and seamlessly integrated into the standard data-gathering/getting-to-know-your-client phase of the engagement (example below).

The gratitude exercise includes the following instructions for use in the first two case examples:

1. Reflect on a person who made a positive contribution to your life.
2. Write a thoughtful, clear, and brief letter to the person (approximately 300 words).
3. Describe their contribution, how it impacted you at the time, and what it means to you today.
4. Reach out to the person and arrange a call or visit.
5. During the meeting, read the letter and spend time talking about the event and your relationship to the person.

In multigenerational family, family business, and non-family business contexts, the gratitude exercise could be adapted by changing the first step, Reflect on a person who made a positive contribution to your life, and by removing the fourth step and having the family members read their letters aloud to each other in the meeting. In the fourth use case example, one or more gratitude-related questions can be incorporated into client questionnaires and/or interviews by simply asking: "With regard to your financial life, who has had the most positive impact on your development?"

Exercise 32: Three Good Things

In the Three Good Things Exercise, clients are asked to spend a week where each night, before they go to sleep, they write down three things that went well for them during the day while reflecting on why they went well.[8] The Three Good Things Exercise instructions are as follows:

1. For the next week, at the end of each day, write down three things that went well and why they went well.

   1. _____

   2. _____

   3. _____

2. At the end of the week, look for patterns in your observations and how they relate to your values and/or goals.

Notes

1. Archuleta, K. L., Grable, J. E., and Burr, E. A. (2015). Solution-focused financial therapy. In B. T. Klontz, S. L. Britt, and K. L. Archuleta (Eds.), *Financial Therapy: Theory, Research, and Practice* (pp. 121–129). Cham: Springer.
2. Ibid.
3. Klontz, B. T., Chaffin, C., and Klontz, P. T. (2023). *Psychology of Financial Planning: The Practitioner's Guide to Money and Behavior.* Hoboken, NJ: Wiley.
4. Mauss, I. B., Tamir, M., Anderson, C. L., and Savino, N. S. (2011). Can seeking happiness make people unhappy? Paradoxical effects of valuing happiness. *Emotion,* 11 (4), pp. 807–815.
5. Snyder, C. R., and Lopez, S. J. (Eds.). (2005). *Handbook of Positive Psychology.* New York: Oxford University Press.
6. Asebedo, S. D., and Seay, M. C. (2015). From functioning to flourishing: Applying positive psychology to financial planning. *Journal of Financial Planning,* 28(11), pp. 50–58.
7. Seligman, M. E. (2012). *Flourish: A Visionary New Understanding of Happiness and Well-Being.* New York: Simon & Schuster.
8. Asebedo, S. D., Seay, M. C., Little, T. D., Enete, S., and Gray, B. (2020). Three good things or three good financial things? Applying a positive psychology intervention to the personal finance domain. *The Journal of Positive Psychology.* doi: 10.1080/17439760.2020.1752779.

Chapter 11

Behavioral Finance: Understanding Cognitive Biases and Heuristics . . . and What to Do About Them

Behavioral finance seeks to understand people's instincts regarding money and, at the risk of oversimplification, figure out why they tend to make poor financial decisions. It examines how *normal* human cognitive processes influence, explain, and predict individual and collective financial behaviors.

A cognitive bias is a systematic error in thinking that arises from our attempts to make sense of a complicated world. Many of these ways of thinking helped us survive and thrive throughout human history. However, in today's complex world, cognitive biases can result in errors in thinking, perception, memory, and attention. A heuristic is a process for doing something, in many cases defined as a rule of thumb that may or may not be ideal but is a readily accessible strategy to solve a problem or analyze a situation. A heuristic tends to be based on previous experiences.

While the thoughts, emotions, and behaviors of clients may vary widely, there are common cognitive biases and heuristics that inform human behavior when it comes to financial decision making. These biases are the result of genetic coding passed down from our ancient ancestors, inborn instincts, and how we, as human beings, perceive the world around us.

There are several steps a financial planner can take to mitigate these biases and help the client stay focused on their long- and short-term goals. At the same time, it is important for the financial planner to recognize their own potential biases. We invite you to reflect on each of these biases as it relates to money to better understand yourself. This inward-facing process will be most helpful so that you may then better help your clients. We discuss the following cognitive biases (and many more) in *Psychology of Financial Planning*.[1] What follows is a brief overview of some of the most prevalent heuristics and biases seen in financial planning with exercises designed to help you identify them within yourself.

Exercise 33: Status Quo Bias

When presented with the opportunity, our brains seek out the path of least resistance. We are inherently lazy, given thousands of years of evolution in selecting the safest and easiest path. To counter this tendency, we can eliminate the friction to help us make changes that will be in our best interests. Since human beings have an innate desire to keep things the same, how can we increase the possibility for success in helping our clients meet their financial goals? One way to address the *status quo bias* is to use that instinctual laziness to the benefit of the client by eliminating the friction and making doing the right thing as easy as possible. For instance, let's say that a client wants to invest more into their retirement. By engaging a financial planner, they have taken the first step in overriding their status quo bias and are excited about taking action to achieve their goal. The client has decided how much they want to contribute each month.

Think of an example in your life where you have eliminated friction to perform a favorable task and one where you had to create friction to limit performing the task.

_____

_____

_____

_____

_____

_____

_____

_____

_____

_____

Exercise 34: Mental Accounting

Mental accounting is placing a disproportionate value on money within different categories. People are prone to categorizing money differently, even though the value of money doesn't change. They put money in mental buckets based on ideas, often irrational. One bucket might be for bills. Another bucket could be a general savings account. A different bucket might be for retirement, but since that seems far away, many people ignore that bucket and leave it empty for much too long. The general savings account bucket is problematic because there is no specific purpose for it. Anytime something comes up, be it car repairs, a big birthday celebration, or a vacation, it's all too easy to dip into that general savings fund.

Think of an example of how mental accounting can be used to assist clients in meeting their financial goals. Can you think of how mental accounting could hurt a client in meeting their goals?

_____

_____

_____

_____

_____

_____

_____

_____

_____

Exercise 35: Endowment Effect

The *endowment effect* is where an individual places a higher value on an object or investment that they already own than the value they would place on it if they did not own it. This is often caused by some emotional attachment to an object, or it is symbolic of something that is especially valuable to the owner. In some cases, the endowment effect occurs merely because we have the object in our possession. The endowment effect is a product of loss aversion. We value what we have, particularly food, water, and shelter to survive.

Think of an object that you own that you probably place a higher value than what it is worth.

_____

_____

_____

_____

_____

_____

_____

_____

_____

Exercise 36: Sunk-Cost Fallacy

The *sunk-cost fallacy* is our tendency to follow through on something even though the costs outweigh the benefits. In financial planning, this often manifests as difficulty letting go of a bad investment or failed business into which we have put our valuable time, energy, and money, regardless of whether the current costs outweigh the benefits. In many cases, the decision to continue with an experience or investment goes against any evidence that suggests that following through is the best decision. It is irrational to consider irrecoverable costs in making a decision in the present. Organizations are also susceptible to the sunk-cost fallacy when they invest in projects that go over budget or even lose their desired objectives partway through the project. Due to their already committed resources, they follow through despite the costs or potential impact.

Think of a project, experience, or relationship where you exhibited the sunk-cost fallacy. Maybe you followed through on a vacation that you didn't enjoy because you prepaid for it or maybe your firm continued a doomed project merely because they made an initial investment. Maybe you held onto a project or relationship long after you knew you should let go. *How can that experience shape helping your clients navigate sunk-cost fallacy?*

_____

_____

_____

_____

_____

_____

_____

_____

_____

_____

Exercise 37: Anchoring Heuristic

Anchoring is an irrational bias toward an arbitrary figure, such as a purchase or listing price, in impacting one's decision making. Anchoring can cause investors to purchase an undervalued investment or sell an overvalued investment. We can avoid anchoring bias by first taking time to evaluate the initial figure that might be contributing to the anchor.

Think of a negotiation where anchoring was used on you to get you to either pay more for something or sell something for less.

_____

_____

_____

_____

_____

_____

_____

_____

_____

_____

Exercise 38: Confirmation Bias

Confirmation bias is a mindset that can hinder our growth and cause harm to ourselves and others. It sifts experiences through the filter of preexisting beliefs. This bias explains the human tendency to seek out evidence to support our beliefs, while simultaneously ignoring or failing to notice evidence that challenges those beliefs.

How can you help a client avoid confirmation bias in the information that you are presenting? This could relate to a marriage and family issue, or to the information that they search on the web.

_____

_____

_____

_____

_____

_____

_____

_____

_____

_____

_____

Note

1. Klontz, B. T., Chaffin, C., and Klontz, P. T. (2023). *Psychology of Financial Planning: The Practitioner's Guide to Money and Behavior.* Hoboken, NJ: Wiley.

Chapter 12

Getting the Client to Take Action

Sometimes clients get stuck at some stage in the financial planning process. Sometimes it is a prospective client who disappears after what you thought was a great first meeting and sometimes it is a longtime client who sits on a decision for months or does not follow through on some aspect of the financial plan. Regardless, it can be one of the most frustrating and time-consuming parts of financial planning.

One of the most powerful psychological techniques that has been adapted for use by financial planners to help their clients take action is motivational interviewing.[1] Motivational interviewing has been used in financial planning to help clients make positive change without the professional confronting or lecturing about the problem behaviors.[2] Lecturing can only make the problem worse, so developing ways to prompt the client to make changes can be a powerful tool in getting them to make decisions and take action on their financial plan.

Exercise 39: Motivational Interviewing Exercise

Goals can be classified in two types: intrinsic and extrinsic.[3] Extrinsic goals involve the pursuit of external rewards (e.g., money) for the purposes of obtaining positive evaluations from others (e.g., social status, popularity). They are focused on the external world. Research has found that the pursuit of extrinsic goals is more stressful and does not lead to the satisfaction of one's needs.[4,5] In contrast, intrinsic goals satisfy our psychological needs innately, because they are focused on what matters most. This includes values-based goals such as autonomy, connection with others, personal growth, and competence.[6,7]

It is not uncommon to find ourselves feeling stuck around an issue. Due to our ambivalence around making a change, our behaviors and values do not always match up. When this happens, it creates tension and leads to lower life satisfaction. We feel out of integrity. We feel like we are not being true to ourselves. What matters most to us is out of sync with how we are behaving. Rather than being rare, the disconnect between our values and our behaviors is quite common.

Here are some examples:

- We value *adventure*, but we haven't taken a vacation in years.
- We value *autonomy*, but we are financially dependent on someone else.
- We love a good *challenge*, but we find ourselves in a routine and stagnant job.
- We value *family*, but we often miss time with family because we are at work.
- We value *generosity*, but we are not giving the way we would like to.
- We value *health*, but we are not eating well or exercising enough.
- We value *honesty*, but we hide our true feelings from our spouse/partner out of fear.
- We value *spirituality,* but we do not engage in any spiritual practices.

Values Versus Behaviors

When we are experiencing problems in our lives, it is usually because of our behaviors and not our values. The great news is that values are often deeply held. They are not fickle. They do not change much over time. Their resilience stands in stark contrast to our behaviors. In comparison to values, behaviors are quite flexible. With the proper motivation, behaviors can be changed instantly. When our behaviors are not in line with our values and we are motivated to ease the discomfort this misalignment creates, it is much easier to change our behaviors.

Since values carry so much motivational potential, it can be helpful to focus on them when someone is struggling with a disconnect between their values and their behaviors. As facilitators, when a client is feeling stuck, it can be tempting to focus on their behaviors. Perhaps they should do more of this. Perhaps they should do less of that. Perhaps they could try this technique. However, there is great value in focusing on a client's values. This could entail helping a client identify and/or remember their values. It could involve conversations meant to strengthen the client's conviction to their values by bringing them into conscious awareness. The facilitator's objective is to heighten the discrepancy between a client's values and behaviors by emphasizing their values.

This exercise can be done with a client, but we recommend you do it yourself first.

1. Identify a disconnect between behaviors and values in conversation with a client or via self-reflection.

_____

_____

_____

_____

_____

_____

_____

_____

_____

2. Specifically identify the behavior and the values. For example, "*I value financial freedom but I'm not saving enough for retirement.*"

_____

_____

_____

_____

_____

_____

_____

_____

_____

_____

3. Through conversation or self-reflection, dive deeper into the value:

- What does it mean?

_____

_____

_____

_____

_____

_____

_____

_____

_____

- Why is it important?

_____

_____

_____

_____

_____

_____

_____

_____

_____

- How does it feel to have a mismatch between your behaviors and your values?

_____

_____

_____

_____

_____

_____

_____

_____

- How would it feel to be actively pursuing this value?

_____

_____

_____

_____

_____

_____

_____

_____

- How do you make sense of yourself with X value and Y behaviors?

_____

_____

_____

_____

_____

_____

_____

_____

_____

4. Rather than focusing on changing behaviors, spend time exploring, fleshing out, and reinforcing the importance of the value.

_____

_____

_____

_____

_____

_____

_____

_____

_____

_____

5. See what happens!

_____

_____

_____

_____

_____

_____

_____

_____

_____

_____

Exercise 40: Well-Done Exercise

The purpose of this exercise is to increase the client's motivation to engage in helpful financial behaviors that go against their natural programming.

- Take 5 to 10 minutes to imagine the following:
  - You are at the end of your life.
  - During your very last conscious moment, imagine that you are able to say "I did it! I accomplished my most important goals."

- Where are you?

_____

_____

_____

_____

_____

_____

_____

_____

- Who is with you?

_____

_____

_____

_____

_____

_____

_____

_____

- What is your financial situation?

  _____

  _____

  _____

  _____

  _____

  _____

  _____

  _____

  _____

- What are you able to say "I did it" about? List the three most important things you were able to accomplish.

  1. _____

  2. _____

  3. _____

- How would you answer a descendant who asked you how you managed to make that happen?

  _____

  _____

  _____

  _____

  _____

Exercise 41: Professional Relationship Forensic Audit

One of our greatest fears is the fear of not belonging. In our ancestors' world, those who didn't belong didn't survive, because without being valued by the tribe, survival was impossible. We still have that need, which permeates much of our daily lives. The fear of being marginalized is even more pronounced in the area of money, where feelings of shame, fear, and anxiety seem to be ubiquitous.

Imagine a situation where you are in your car, waiting in line to make a turn, when suddenly, someone cuts in line ahead of you without warning or without asking permission. Notice the feelings that arise even in this hypothetical scenario. Unfortunately, in many cases, people act out those feelings. It is called road rage.

Imagine now, being in the same line, that someone comes up beside you, with their blinker on, and with a pleading look that "begs" to be allowed to go in front and you let them in. You will have an entirely different feeling.

What's the difference?

In both cases, you are now one more car back. The person who cut you off, through their actions of pretending that you didn't exist, triggered that ancient "not-belonging" fear. They, by their actions, have said "you are insignificant" or "as far as I'm concerned, you do not exist." To our ancestors, such a slight meant a threat to our social standing and survival, and our ancestors would fight to regain their place. In the second scenario, our feelings are different because the person now in front of us identified us as the leader who had thumbs-up/thumbs-down power over their lives. By asking you, they have acknowledged your value as a human being, the safest place in tribal society. This may seem silly in today's world, but the part of the

Psychology of Financial Planning: Practitioner's Toolkit

brain that is most involved in this drama has not received a programming update in thousands of years.

Assign a number from 0 to 5 to the following statements, where 0 = Not true at all and 5 = Totally true. Put yourself in the perspective of one of your own clients meeting with you in person at your office if you are a practicing financial planner or, if you are not, from the perspective of you as a client (e.g., of a CPA, financial planner, attorney, etc.).

_____ 1. When I call, you would personally answer my call.

_____ 2. If you couldn't answer, I would have an opportunity to leave a message on your personal voicemail.

_____ 3. In the voicemail message, I would hear your voice.

_____ 4. Typically, you personally (rather than an assistant) would return my call within 24 hours.

_____ 5. When I enter the building where your office is located, the dominant physical features I first encounter would consist of wood and/or stone, or artwork/furnishings that feature the same.

_____ 6. You would meet me at your office building's outer door.

_____ 7. Once inside your office, I would find hot and/or room temperature/cold beverages served in ceramic or glass containers available for me.

_____ 8. I could count on you to stop doing everything else (meetings, phone calls, emails, texts, Facebook, trolling the internet etc.) at least 20 minutes before our scheduled meeting or call so you would be focused on me and not distracted.

_____ 9. When I walked into your office, I would be free to choose where I sat.

_____ 10. Once in your office, we would sit with nothing between us.

_____ 11. Typically, you would not be taking notes but would be looking at me while we talked.

_____ 12. The furniture in your office would have rounded edges.

_____ 13. Your office space would be vetted or staged by someone familiar with interior decorating.

_____ 14. Typically, you would avoid asking me questions during our time together.

_____ 15. You would employ a variety of sensory tools to help explain important concepts or to show me that you understood what I was saying.

_____ 16. Our sessions, if they were recorded and analyzed, would show that for the length of time we were together, 75% of the time you were listening to me, 20% of the time you were reflecting or summarizing what you heard me say, and 5% of the time you would be sharing your expertise and advice.

_____ 17. That same analysis would show that you summarized what I said four times as often as you made a request for more information from me.

_____ 18. We would start with my agenda rather than yours.

_____ 19. I would get a surprise personal communication/interaction from you occasionally, just checking to see how I'm doing and letting me know you are thinking of me.

_____ 20. Communications from you are almost always personalized.

_____ **Total Score (100 points possible)**

Your total score represents the degree to which your interactions with your clients help reduce their anxiety and, at the same time, increase the likelihood that your meetings with them will have optimal results.

Nine Evidence-Based Techniques for Overcoming Client Resistance to Financial Advice

In *Psychology of Financial Planning: The Practitioner's Guide to Money and Behavior,*[8] we present nine evidence-based motivation-enhancing communication techniques that can be used with clients who are resisting our advice. The key is to critically evaluate your current strategy and consider the following nine steps. Before each statement is a detailed definition of the technique and how it can be used in practice.

Exercise 42: Simple Reflection

Like a mirror, this technique involves reflecting the client's statements and assertions with as much accuracy as possible. The planner should be selective about which parts to reflect to the client, often choosing the things the client says that are in support of the desired change, when offered by the client. Financial planners can reflect back a statement or an emotion that the client is sharing.

Client: "I know I have been putting off this estate planning stuff. I just don't want to deal with it all."

Planner: _____

_____

_____

_____

Exercise 43: Complex Reflection

With a complex reflection, the planner takes an educated guess about where the client is going. It can feel like trying to complete the client's sentence. If the guess is accurate, the client feels even more understood. If it is inaccurate, the client can correct you and get to the heart of the matter.

Client: "I know I have been putting off this estate planning stuff. I just don't want to deal with it all."

Planner: _____

_____

_____

_____

Exercise 44: Amplified Reflection

When a planner uses this technique, they will reflect an extreme version of the client's message. It's human nature to correct an exaggeration. Through the their tendency to correct the amplified reaction, the client often finds themself arguing in favor of making the desired change, rather than fighting against it.

Client: "I know I have been putting off this estate planning stuff. I just don't want to deal with it all."

Planner: _____

_____

_____

_____

Exercise 45: Double-Sided Reflection

This technique can help the client explore the pros and cons of taking action. When the planner reflects both sides of the client's ambivalence, the client is liberated from feeling pressured to argue for the status quo.

Client: "I know I have been putting off this estate planning stuff. I just don't want to deal with it all."

Planner: _____

_____

_____

_____

Exercise 46: Shifting the Focus from What's Not Working to What Is Working

When a client is showing resistance to a financial planner's advice, sometimes it makes sense to shift the focus away from the impasse. When a person is hyperfocused on maintaining the status quo, it might be indicative of them being in a precontemplative state of change.

Client: "I know I have been putting off this estate planning stuff. I just don't want to deal with it all."

Psychology of Financial Planning: Practitioner's Toolkit

Planner: _____

_____

_____

_____

Exercise 47: Reframing

When we are feeling stuck, it can help to look at an issue from a different angle. With the technique of reframing, we are attempting to offer up an alternative meaning to a situation. By looking at an issue through a different lens, clients may be able to better receive new information and can generate new solutions.

Client: "I know I have been putting off this estate planning stuff. I just don't want to deal with it all."

Planner: _____

_____

_____

_____

Exercise 48: Agreement with a Twist

People relax when they feel others agree with them. They aren't as determined to prove a point and that makes them more receptive to what others have to say. This technique involves agreeing with the client and then adding a twist that will redirect the client away from resistance. In other words, it combines agreeing with the client and normalizing their experience, followed by a reframe. When the client feels validated, they are more willing to accept new ideas.

Client: "I know I have been putting off this estate planning stuff. I just don't want to deal with it all."

Getting the Client to Take Action

Planner: _____

_____

_____

_____

Exercise 49: Emphasizing Self-Determination

Nobody likes being told what to do. When a financial planner notices signs of resistance in a client, it might make sense to honor and support the part of the client that is seeking to gain control and assert their independence. Clients who feel like they are in control and in charge of their choices will be less resistant to change.

Client: "I know I have been putting off this estate planning stuff. I just don't want to deal with it all."

Planner: _____

_____

_____

_____

Exercise 50: Arguing Against Change

This powerful technique may seem counterintuitive, but it can be quite effective when used at the right time and delivered skillfully. This is not like "reverse psychology," which is used to trick people into choosing the thing they are resisting. This technique can take several forms, including "go slow" messages, which paradoxically, often make people want to move faster. The planner must be willing to support the client's choice to not make a change that could improve their lives, trusting that the client is making the decision they think is best for them at this time. If the planner perceives that the client is being motivated by external forces, like appeasing a demanding family member, this technique may guide the client back to their intrinsic motivation. Siding with the client's opposition to change can externalize their ambivalence in the opposite direction, with the advisor taking the side of the status quo. It may even help remind them why they decided to seek the help of a financial planner in the first place.

Client: "I know I have been putting off this estate planning stuff. I just don't want to deal with it all."

Planner: _____

_____

_____

_____

Notes

1. Miller, W. R., and Rollnick, S. (2012). *Motivational Interviewing: Helping People Change* (3rd ed.). New York: The Guilford Press.
2. Klontz, B., Kahler, R., and Klontz, T. (2016). *Facilitating Financial Health Tools for Financial Planners, Coaches, and Therapists* (2nd ed.). The National Underwriter Company.
3. Kasser, T., and Ryan, R. M. (1996). Further examining the American dream: Differential correlates of intrinsic and extrinsic goals. *Personality and Social Psychology Bulletin*, 22, pp. 280–287.
4. Ibid.
5. Sheldon, K. M., and Kasser, T. (1995). Coherence and congruence: Two aspects of personality integration. *Journal of Personality and Social Psychology*, 68, pp. 531–543.
6. Deci, E. L., and Ryan, R. M. (1985). *Intrinsic Motivation and Self-Determination in Human Behavior*. New York: Plenum Press.
7. Maslow, A. H. (1954). *Motivation and Personality*. New York: Harper & Row.
8. Klontz, B. T., Chaffin, C., and Klontz, P. T. (2023). *Psychology of Financial Planning: The Practitioner's Guide to Money and Behavior*. Hoboken, NJ: Wiley.

Getting the Client to Take Action

Going Forward

We invite you to visit www.PsychologyOfFinancialPlanning.com to learn about our continuing education offerings, workshops, and ways that we can continue to work together in the future. We hope that this toolkit has helped you in better understanding yourself, your own biases, financial flashpoints, and cultural competence. For most people, some of the questions included in this book can uncover some new and exciting takeaways about ourselves and what motivates us, as well as how we see the world and the people around us. All of these takeaways have implications for our practice and how we engage our clients on a daily basis.

Exercise 51: Your Takeaways

Before you go, based on the knowledge and skills you have learned here, consider the following questions:

- What did you learn about yourself?
- What did you learn about your clients?
- How will you adjust your approach to working with clients in the future?
- What next steps can you take to further your education in the area of the psychology of financial planning?
- What are your three biggest takeaways from this book?

    1. _____

    2. _____

    3. _____

In Closing

Integrating psychology into financial planning requires a clear understanding of the boundaries between the roles of a financial planner and a mental health provider. These boundaries are important for many reasons, including the need to abide by the strict ethical codes that have been established in the mental health profession. We describe these in detail in the accompanying book, *Psychology of Financial Planning*. However, they are so important that we included an excerpt here.

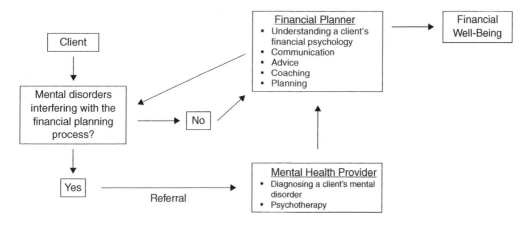

This illustration is designed to highlight the difference between the role of the financial planner and that of a mental health professional. *It is critical to understand that a financial planner is* not *a mental health provider.* In fact, it would be unethical for a mental health provider, acting in their role as a mental health provider, to also manage their client's money. As such, when a client is exhibiting mental health–related concerns – including a money disorder (e.g., compulsive buying disorder), anxiety, or depression – a financial planner would not attempt to "treat" the client. When a client exhibits signs of a mental disorder, the financial planner should consider making a referral to a mental health provider who can diagnose and treat the potential disorder. The financial planner would never attempt to "diagnose" a client, but rather make a referral because the client is exhibiting behaviors that appear to be impairing their functioning in one or more areas of their life (e.g. emotional, occupational, and/or relational functioning) and are getting in the way of the financial planning process. The referral could happen at the beginning of the financial planning process or at some point later in the relationship.

When and How to Refer

A financial planner will often make referrals to other professionals, such as a CPA, an estate planning attorney, or an insurance specialist. At some point a financial planner is also likely to encounter times when the best option would be to refer their client to a mental health provider. For instance, if a client is experiencing panic attacks related to their financial concerns, a referral to a mental health provider may be in order. The client will not be able to hear or follow through on the planner's recommendations if they are in a state of acute anxiety. It is reasonable for the planner to postpone tackling certain aspects of the financial planning process until the client is getting help for their anxiety, or they may decide to work in tandem with a mental health provider, depending on the severity of the client's needs.

The best way to know when to refer a client is if they seem stuck and the planner has run out of all the tools they are qualified to use. A planner who understands their client's financial psychology, is comfortable with a client expressing emotions, is a good listener, and can skillfully employ one or more of the communication and counseling tactics in this book may be able to help facilitate behavioral change in their client. However, despite a financial planner's best efforts, some clients may struggle to move forward and/or keep engaging in financially self-destructive behaviors despite the consequences.

Some indicators that it may be time to refer the client to a mental health provider include the following:

- Severe symptoms of depression or anxiety
- Addiction, compulsive behaviors, or money disorders
- A history of trauma surrounding money
- A chronic inability to implement financial plans or change destructive behaviors

- High conflict between couples and/or families

- A chronic inability to communicate openly and transparently about finances

- Other mental health issues that are negatively impacting a client's emotional, occupational, or social abilities and functioning

It is important to use discretion when deciding whether to refer a client to a psychotherapist. The planner should refrain from making assumptions about the client based only on the circumstances. A client with a previous money disorder, for example, may be at a place in their life where they are ready to make the necessary changes based on the financial planner's recommendations. A skilled planner may be the right professional to guide the client out of their old behaviors and into a healthier course of action. That is why it is crucial for a planner to consider the client's behaviors, emotions, and history, as well as their own reactions and emotions.

If the planner is feeling uncomfortable, fearful, or nervous around a client, it is a good indicator that they should consider bringing in another professional to help. Sometimes referring a client to someone else is the best thing a planner can do for them. It is important for the planner to understand that making a referral does not equal quitting or an admission of incompetence. Rather, it is a sign that the planner is skilled and practiced enough to recognize the signs that the client would benefit from the expertise of a professional from a different field. During every interaction, whether the planner decides to refer or not, the client's needs and well-being should be paramount.

Ethical Considerations

The psychology of financial planning requires the planner to be aware of what is happening inside the client's mind. While it can be beneficial for a planner to understand a client's psychology, it is important for financial planners to understand their own professional limitations. A planner can distinguish the appropriate guidelines and boundaries around inner psychological work with clients by examining the Ethical Principles of Psychologists and Code of Conduct for the American Psychological Association[1] and the Code of Ethics and Professional Responsibility for the Certified Financial Planner[2] Board of Standards.[3] Both codes require that a practitioner work only within the boundaries of their professional competence.

Another critical ethical consideration for mental health practitioners is to avoid *multiple relationships* with clients.[4] It would be unethical for someone acting in the role of a mental health therapist to also work in the role of financial planner with the same client – even if they are qualified to do both. To protect clients and maintain the sanctity of the mental health therapist-client relationship, the mental health provider must avoid having such multiple relationships with their clients, as it could put their clients at risk. For example, if a person and/or a firm is providing mental health therapy *and* financial planning to the same client, what if a client relies on their therapeutic support but is unhappy with the financial planning element? To maintain the therapeutic relationship, which may be essential to their mental health stability, they might feel compelled to stay with the financial planning component even though they believe that doing so is no longer in their best interest. This type of situation puts the client's best interests at risk, which is why it is strictly forbidden under mental health practitioner ethical guidelines.

Conclusion

We hope that the exercises in this book, and the information in its companion, *Psychology of Financial Planning: Practitioner's Guide to Money and Behavior*, provide you with the insights and tools you need to integrate the psychology of financial planning into your work with clients. We hope they provide you with a better understanding of your financial psychology so you can better engage and serve clients from diverse backgrounds to improve their lives in meaningful ways.

Notes

1. American Psychological Association. (2017). *APA Ethical Principles of Psychologists and Code of Conduct, Ethical Standard 2.01: Boundaries of Competence.* Washington, DC: American Psychological Association.
2. CFP Board. (2022). *Code of Ethics and Standards of Conduct.* Available at: https://www.cfp.net/ethics/code-of-ethics-and-standards-of-conduct.
3. Klontz, B., Kahler, R., and Klontz, T. (2016). Doing no harm. In *Facilitating Financial Health: Tools for Financial Planners, Coaches, and Therapists* (2nd ed., pp. 35–46). The National Underwriter Company.
4. American Psychological Association. (2017). *APA Ethical Principles of Psychologists and Code of Conduct, Ethical Standard 2.01: Boundaries of Competence.* Washington, DC: American Psychological Association.

Index

Page numbers followed by *f* refer to figures.

Goals, 29f, 53f, 173
Gordon, Thomas, 103
Gratitude Exercise, 157–158

H
Happiness, 155
Hays, Pamela, 21
Heuristics, 163, 167–168
Hoarding, 84–85

I
Immigration, 31
Incomplete Sentences Intervention, 6–14
Indigenous heritage, clients with, 22
Instincts, financial, 29f, 53f

K
Kinesthetic learners, 112–113
Klontz-Chaffin Model of Financial Psychology, 29f, 53f
Klontz Money Behavior Inventory (KMBI), 80–91
Klontz Money Script Inventory--Revised (KMSI-R), 54–61

L
Learning Style Exercise, 113–114
Learning styles, 111–114
Listening, 105–107, 114
Listening by Sketch (exercise), 106–107
Logical learners, 112

M
Majority status, 20–26
Mealtime, 92
Mental accounting, 165
Mental health providers, financial planners vs., 193–196
Mindfulness Meditation, 91–93
Minority status, 20–26
Miracle Question (exercise), 153–154
Money avoidance, 58–60
Money conflict, 121–144
Money Egg (exercise), 46–49f, 46–50
Money focus, 60

Money Script Log, 61–67, 154
Money scripts, 29, 29f, 53–73, 53f
Money status, 58–60
Money vigilance, 58–59, 61
Motivational interviewing, 173–189
Motivational Interviewing Exercise, 173–179
Motivations, attitudes, and preferences, 29f, 53f
Multicultural competence, 19–26
Multicultural Experience (exercise), 19–20
Multiple relationships, avoiding, 196

N
National origin, client's, 22, 23
New Money Mantra (exercise), 67–72, 154

O
Open-Ended Invitation (exercise), 97–99
Outcomes, financial, 77–93

P
Principles of counseling, 153–159
Professional Relationship Forensic Audit, 182–184
Psychology, positive, 157
Psychology of Financial Planning (Klontz, Chaffin, and Klontz), 147, 153, 163, 184, 193, 196

Q
Question-Free Zone Exercise, 100–103

R
Racial identity, client's, 22
Reading/writing learners, 112
Reflection, 98–100
Reflection Exercise, 100
Reframing, 187
Relationships, avoiding multiple, 196
Religion, client's, 21, 22
Retirement, 5

S
Self-awareness, 137–144
Self-efficacy Reflection, 14–15
75% Rule, 114–116

Printed and bound by CPI Group (UK) Ltd, Croydon, CR0 4YY

13/01/2025

14625378-0001